Kevin J. Gardner is Associate Professor of English at Baylor University in Waco, Texas. A Betjeman scholar, he is the author of *Betjeman and the Anglican Imagination* (SPCK, 2010). He is also the editor of *Faith and Doubt of John Betjeman: An anthology of his religious verse* (Continuum, 2005) and *Poems in the Porch: The radio poems of John Betjeman* (Continuum, 2008). In addition to his work on Betjeman, he has published on a wide variety of literary figures over the years, and has a particular interest in twentieth-century writers who address issues of faith and religion.

BETJEMAN ON FAITH

An anthology of his religious prose

Edited by Kevin J. Gardner

First published in Great Britain in 2011

Society for Promoting Christian Knowledge
36 Causton Street
London SW1P 4ST
www.spckpublishing.co.uk

Preface copyright © Kevin J. Gardner 2011
All other chapters copyright © the Estate of Sir John Betjeman 2011

Scripture quotations are taken from the Authorized Version of the Bible (The King James Bible),
the rights in which are vested in the Crown, and are reproduced by permission of
the Crown's Patentee, Cambridge University Press.
Extracts from The Book of Common Prayer, the rights in which are vested in the
Crown, are reproduced by permission of the Crown's Patentee, Cambridge
University Press.

British Library Cataloguing-in-Publication Data
A catalogue record for this book is available from the British Library

ISBN 978–0–281–06416–8

1 3 5 7 9 10 8 6 4 2

Typeset by Graphicraft Ltd, Hong Kong
Printed in Great Britain by Ashford Colour Press

Produced on paper from sustainable forests

*To Hilary
and to Graham*

'I long for Jesus as a Man, I long to see Him, to be lifted up to Him, to love Him, not to injure Him as much as I do all the time. I *try* to long for Him when I don't long for Him. Jesus is the centre of my faith and the Sacraments are one of the ways by which I try to know Him.'

Letter to Penelope Betjeman, 2 June 1949

Contents

❦

Part 1
FAITH AND CULTURE

Part 2
CHRISTIAN AESTHETICS

Part 3
CHURCHES AND CATHEDRALS

Part 4
THE CHRISTIAN LIFE

Part 5
BELIEF AND DOUBT

Preface

Poet, journalist, broadcaster, preservationist and beloved icon of Englishness: to John Betjeman these successes meant nothing without his faith. Underlying everything he wrote and all he campaigned for was an encompassing Christian commitment that to him meant a regular observance of the sacraments, a lifelong spiritual struggle to merit salvation, and an aesthetic pleasure in the material culture of Anglicanism. As he admitted to Evelyn Waugh, 'Of course, upbringing, habit, environment, connections – all sorts of worldly things – make me love the C. of E. But this would not matter a straw, if I *knew*, in the Pauline sense, that Our Lord was not present at an Anglican Mass.'[1] Faith, complex and serious, was not compartmentalized and separated from his public life. The struggle to sustain his faith and invigorate his church infuses every genre in which he wrote: poetry and letters, essays and journalism, radio broadcasts and television films. Unabashedly revealing his personal beliefs and doubts, he explored theological dilemmas that challenge rational thinkers, argued for the interconnectedness of religion and the arts, discussed the dependence of English society on its established Church, instructed his readers about the life and history of parishes and church buildings, and in moving elegies lamented the loss of churches. He is without doubt one of the most important voices of faith and culture in the twentieth century.

To read Betjeman today is to discover a mind profoundly engaged with a striking variety of topics pertaining to Christian faith and experience. Questions of belief were inescapable for him, and they remain so for anyone who reads Betjeman closely. This volume is sure to portray the more sombre aspects of Betjeman's personality, easily manifested by a sudden recollection of his own mortality or of the uncertainty of eternity. Though religion was a subject of great seriousness to him, it did not always prevent him from injecting a note of humour into a portentous topic. There were parish 'arguments about cow parsley on the altar', for instance, which he includes among those cherished hallmarks of Englishness

---

[1] Quotations from Betjeman's letters throughout this volume are from *John Betjeman: Letters*, Vol. 1, ed. Candida Lycett Green (London: Methuen, 1994).

most under threat of imminent Nazi invasion.[2] Or there was St Endellion Church, which looked 'just like a hare', yet whose architecture, history and spiritual mystery were worth serious attention.[3] Such memorable whimsy typifies Betjeman's voice, and is rarely absent except in moments of the most sober reflection. Not surprisingly, superficial pleasures can open the door to seriousness, as he admits in a 1937 letter to Alan Pryce-Jones: 'The thing that has happened to me is that after years of sermon tasting, I am now a member of the C. of E. and a communicant. I regard it as the only salvation against progress and Fascists on the one side and Marxists of Bloomsbury on the other.'

Indeed, surprise is one of the great experiences in reading the work of John Betjeman. 'Who knew what undiscovered glories hung/Waiting in locked-up churches', he wrote in his autobiographical poem.[4] The same question could be asked of the archives holding Betjeman's papers. For many the most surprising undiscovered glory in this book may be the sermon he preached at St Matthew's Church, Northampton, on 5 May 1946. Privately printed in a slim volume with sermons preached there by other laymen, Betjeman's sermon is a homiletical masterpiece that suggests an alternative career in the Church had he been so inclined. However, the anxiety he felt determined him not to accept future such requests. Perhaps it was stage fright before a congregation of 600, perhaps it was the distress of having to follow in the pulpit his old Oxford tutor and antagonist, C. S. Lewis. Despite his misgivings, his sermon is rhetorically powerful and theologically substantive, a work of both beauty and humility – and also not without its wry moments of self-deprecating humour. It contains some of the most affective prose that he ever composed and is moreover a deeply personal revelation.

This sermon is surely my most fortuitous discovery about Betjeman and remains for me the central text of this collection, which grew out of original research that I was conducting for my book, *Betjeman and the Anglican Imagination* (London: SPCK, 2010). It was while preparing to write that book that I began to realize that religion was not simply one of Betjeman's many interests but the central preoccupation of his life, and one that influenced his thinking on all other matters. In his poetry, Betjeman's explorations of faith and doubt and his celebrations of the life of the Church are relatively well known, but perhaps this is rather less the

---

[2] '"Oh, to be in England . . ."', *The Listener*, 11 March 1943, p. 296.
[3] See pp. 94–7 of this volume.
[4] *Summoned by Bells* (London: John Murray, 1960), p. 48.

case with his prose. Until now, much of Betjeman's religious prose has remained uncollected, available only to readers with access to microform, out-of-print books, and archives. This anthology of Betjeman's religious prose is intended to reveal the great diversity of his thinking and writing on the subjects of the spiritual and social natures of Christianity.

Scholarship can be a lonely business, so it is gratifying to have made the acquaintance and earned the respect of other writers devoted to Betjeman. As always, I am profoundly grateful to Bevis Hillier for his friendship and encouragement and especially for laying the foundation for all my work on Betjeman. His magisterial biographical trilogy continues to inspire and impress me, and all scholars of the life and writings of Betjeman owe Bevis a debt of gratitude. I must also acknowledge two other scholars whose work has made this anthology possible. Bill Peterson's *John Betjeman: A bibliography* (Oxford: Clarendon Press, 2006) made the identification and location of Betjeman's more obscure prose a much less exhausting task, and Stephen Games identified several interesting pieces and graciously provided me with copies from his own collection. I deeply admire their scholarship, and I remain grateful for their support, advice and assistance.

For her immediate interest in this book, and for overseeing it through to publication, I am grateful to my editor at SPCK, Alison Barr. Also of invaluable support at SPCK were Mark Casserley, Rima Devereaux, Lauren Zimmerman and the editorial and production teams. Thanks also to copy-editor Steve Gove. During the early stages of editing this book I benefited from the research assistance of Louise North at the BBC's Written Archives Centre, John Frederick of the Betjeman Archive at the McPherson Library of the University of Victoria, and Georgiana Vear at the *Daily Telegraph*, and I am indebted to them for their kind help. I am also grateful for the support of Dr Truell Hyde, Vice Provost for Research at Baylor University, who generously provided me with an Arts and Humanities Faculty Development grant to assist with research-related costs. And finally I wish to express my gratitude to the Estate of the late Sir John Betjeman for their permission to publish and their encouragement of this project.

Further reading

The best single-volume biographical source is Bevis Hillier's *John Betjeman: The biography* (London: John Murray, 2006), effectively an abridgement of his three-volume trilogy published between 1988 and 2004. The best of Betjeman's religious poems are available in two anthologies that I have edited: *Faith and Doubt of John Betjeman: An anthology of his religious verse* (London: Continuum, 2005) and *Poems in the Porch: The radio poems of John Betjeman* (London: Continuum, 2008). Those wishing to read a detailed analysis of Betjeman's Christian imagination are directed to my book, *Betjeman and the Anglican Imagination* (London: SPCK, 2010), while those who might wish to consult some shorter analyses are directed to the following sources: my introduction to *Faith and Doubt* (cited above), my article 'Anglicanism and the Poetry of John Betjeman' (*Christianity and Literature* 53.3 (2004), pp. 361–83), Peter J. Lowe's article 'The Church as a Building and the Church as a Community in the Work of John Betjeman' (*Christianity and Literature* 57.4 (2008), pp. 559–81), and Stephen Games's introduction to *Sweet Songs of Zion* (London: Hodder and Stoughton, 2007).

Part 1

FAITH AND CULTURE

'Now I quite agree with you that the Church is imperfect, that many problems can be solved and aren't solved because of human slackness and weakness. . . . But I know that Christianity is not a negative force but may even do some service by immunizing people against worse creeds, such as Fascism. I believe it's positive and can alone save the world, not from Fascism, or Nazism, but from evil.'

Letter to Roy Harrod, 25 March 1939

Oh, for a faith

from *Ghastly Good Taste* (1933)

I am pleasantly awoken every morning in London by the sound of a church bell at eight o'clock. It sounds above the early lorries and rides triumphant over the roaring engines being warmed up in the garage of the street behind me, before the chauffeurs depart to fetch their precious masters to the office. And every morning as this bell rings, one elderly sexton, two old ladies and a pale youth attend the daily communion – or mass, as it is called among Anglo-Catholics – in St Agatha's. During the day the church remains open, and some more old women and some

> Young men, that no one knows, go in and out
> With a far look in their eternal eyes.

But out of every 500 people who go down my street, I do not think it would be inaccurate to say that less than three call in at St Agatha's. When the bell rings and wakes me in the morning, even though I am tired, I envy the young man and the two old women and the sexton their faith, that will let them face the discomfort of early rising for a mystic experience in St Agatha's to carry them through the day. That early morning bell is symbolic of the lost age of faith; the symbolism becomes even more pathetic when, twenty minutes after the eight o'clock bell, six strokes on the sanctus tell the people cleaning the gramophone shop and the men at the Lex Garage opposite that the Son of Man died to save the world, and has died again just across the road today....

In the village of Thaxted, in Essex, there has been an attempt, not unsuccessful, to centre the life of the place round the catholic service of the church. The church has become a place of importance once more, not a seedy relic continually needing repairs to the chancel; there is some reason for the numerous footpaths which lead to it, dotted across the ordnance map; and the footpaths are not always straight. Church social life was not originally confined to tea-parties and Dorcas Societies. At Thaxted, the public-house is not looked upon as a place of sin. Yet despite the religious atmosphere of Thaxted church, and despite the communal life centring

3

round it and the able and great character of Conrad Noel, the incumbent, one realizes that it is only in remote agricultural districts that faith, as the medieval Church knew it, stands any chance of surviving. Therefore one cannot blame the canons who lecture and the preservation-mad town councillors and the Wykehamists for treating Gothic architecture in terms of medieval archaeology. Every village with its cottages clustered round its church is a relic. For the cottagers have moved to the towns, and the cottages are filled with arty escapists who are trying to blind themselves with the past, and the workers are in the cinema in Stortford, or on their motor bicycles, or listening to the wireless, or reading Lord Castlerosse or James Douglas in the *Sunday Express*, when the bell for service rings. But do not blame the vicar, he is no longer a man with authority. Blame the age, for that is the only thing which can frighten you. The age has lost one faith, but it does not yet seem to have found another.

Domine dirige nos

The Listener, 9 January 1941

One of the most moving experiences London had to offer before this war was the City on a fine summer evening of a Sunday. Offices were shut, underground trains were infrequent, the sharks had floated away in their limousines on Friday, the streets were empty and the City became the ancient capital of a Christian country. In the late evening light it was easy to imagine that the winding alleys and footpaths between high Victorian office blocks were flanked by overhanging medieval houses, and to add to the illusion there were church bells ringing round every corner. Here and there one saw a few choirboys racing towards the one building that was awake, a neighbouring City church. A single ting-ting from St Alban's, Wood Street, at six, and there was that green gas-lit interior, dusted for Evensong. By a quarter to seven Christ Church, Newgate Street, nearby had started ringing for service while the fuller peals – St Andrew Holborn, St Clement Danes, St Mary-le-Bow – provided deeper and more distant music beneath the single tinkles. And in the streets and from the bridges Sunday re-asserted the forest of chiming towers and steeples, white Portland stone or black, tapering lead, with St Paul's, a mother hen brooding among them, just as before 1666 many more towers and spires were seen from Clerkenwell marshes, gathered round Old St Paul's in Rembrandt's drawing.

Since I was a boy of twelve I have visited the City churches again and again, so that I can remember the interior of every one, for there is not one so dim and so locked that I have not managed to attend a service there. I have even attended a Welsh service for the purpose of getting into St Benet's, Paul's Wharf, one of Wren's best and least known buildings. To the time of writing it has escaped destruction. And it is from sitting in the churches on Sundays, visiting them on weekdays and going to a great deal of trouble to get the key when they were not open, that I have let the impression they made sink into me so that no fire or bombs or business bishop or lazy incumbent can destroy them for me.

One reads the usual paragraphs about the churches the Germans burnt the other night – that Milton lies in St Giles', Cripplegate, Judge Jeffreys in St Mary Aldermanbury, that the Blue Coat boys come back to Christ

Church, once the parish church of Christ's Hospital, to special services, that 'Thomas Ingoldsby' was rector of St Vedast's, Foster Lane. Milton's bones may have been shifted by the Germans, Judge Jeffreys' stone may have cracked and gone, Barham would not recognize St Vedast's and the Blue Coat boys will sit in those high galleries of Christ Church no more. But it was not the well-known names and historic events that made the churches of the City so important, nor even the repeated attempts of certain ecclesiastics to sell the sites, nor even the fact that they had survived the fire, or not survived the fire and been designed by Wren, or survived Wren and been designed by some even better architect, the noble Hawksmoor or delicate George Dance, Junior. The City is about one square mile. Before the fire of 1666 there were 93; Wren rebuilt about 50, and though others were never rebuilt, there were 76 churches in the City in the early nineteenth century. Since that date 25 have been destroyed, and of the 51 that survived the Victorians and the present century, 11 have been almost destroyed by the Germans and another 14 have been damaged with varying degrees of severity.

Nearly every City church, whatever its date, carries with it an atmosphere of cedar-scented pews, richly-cushioned aldermen's chairs, clocks fatly ticking in dark galleries, towering organ lofts and mellow organs, no expense spared on stained glass; and where the clear glass survives it is possible to look through at the sky and think oneself back to the times of the Guilds when London was a dry island among marshes by the Thames, to work through to the days of City companies and merchants consulting turnips while apprentices and charity children looked down from galleries and the rector preached theology in bands. The City churches were Prayer Book architecture, and it is their English texture which has been destroyed and can never be copied. Certainly some of the finer buildings, when Wren was not concerned to wedge as much accommodation as possible into a confined space, can be copied on freer, finer sites. But the small intimate Renaissance interiors like St Vedast's, Foster Lane, are gone forever.

Of the ten buildings which looked to me most ruinous two were among the great interiors of the City, and both were by Wren. St Bride's, Fleet Street, had its old high pews, galleries, organ and clear glass in all its windows except the east one, which was inappropriate and no loss. It was an almost untouched Wren interior. Christ Church, Newgate Street, had fine woodwork and even lovelier was the plaster decoration all over the interior east wall: this survives, but the ceiling is gone and the church is finished. One can only be thankful that the 'cathedral' glass has gone, too.

Fortunately the original steeples of both these churches survive, though St Bride's may well have to come down and be rebuilt – an experience it has suffered before.

Among the other heavy casualties are St Andrew-by-the-Wardrobe, a brick and stone Wren building, plain without, for it was not, when originally built, visible from the street. It had very lovely woodwork, pews and organ case, and reminded one of the hold of an old ship. St Vedast's, Foster Lane, had a Wren steeple of triangular shape, which is to me the most lovely of all in the City. It is still there. St Lawrence Jewry was in every way Wren's finest interior, and if only a bomb had destroyed the Victorian glass and not the magnificent organ case, iron sword-rests, pews and plaster work this would have been the most exquisite Renaissance church in London. The vestry, with its carving, its thick and elaborate plaster work, its painted ceiling, was one of the sights of the City. St Stephen's, Coleman Street, is little architectural loss. 'Restorations' had robbed this plain Wren church of its woodwork and character. St Alban's, Wood Street, the last City church to be lit with gas, was generally locked. It was Wren Gothic 'corrected' by Sir Gilbert Scott into any Victorian suburban church. The tower was square and firm and alone survives. St Anne and St Agnes was modest outside, but it had a most beautiful flat-domed ceiling; one small part of this dome survives. It is an interior worth repairing. St Giles', Cripplegate, was robbed of most of its Renaissance and medieval fittings in the latter part of the last century and now the superb little eighteenth-century painted window has gone and many of the monuments. The Perpendicular arcades survive. All Hallows', Barking, another medieval church, was full of treasures, the best of which was the font cover, three cherubs struggling round some fruit, probably the best work of Grinling Gibbons. I should like to know that this has been saved. The Dutch Church at Austin Friars was a Friars' preaching church. It had few fittings, was scraped inside and lit by ugly greenish glass. On its spacious Gothic proportions and the stone floor its later beauty depended, and there is little reason why this church should not arise better from the bombing.

Of the 14 that are damaged, the greatest tragedy is St Mary Abchurch, which had a painted dome by Sir James Thornhill, the father-in-law of Hogarth, a grand carved and festooned pulpit, altarpiece and organ case. The other superb and irreplaceable churches of the 14 which must be repaired are St Mary Woolnoth (by Hawksmoor, Wren's pupil and a more original architect than Wren), St Mary-at-Hill which has the most complete collection of wood and ironwork in the City, St Dunstan's in the East whose 1823 Gothic interior is unique and unspoiled by later generations, and whose spire is Wren at his best, St Magnus the Martyr (Wren), St Stephen's, Walbrook (Wren), St Clement Danes (Wren) and All Hallows', London Wall (George Dance, Junior).

In their pursuit of these important 'military objectives', the Germans have still to destroy St Mildred's, Bread Street, Wren's neatest and completest interior in architecture and fittings, spoiled at present by bad stained glass; St Peter's, Cornhill (Wren), St Botolph's, Aldersgate, George Dance, Junior's, gayest interior, whose east window is rare and beautiful as well as 20 more excellent churches, medieval, Wren and later.

I have heard a story, which may not be true, that when Bristol city was bombed, the clergy of St Mary Redcliffe, its finest Gothic church, stood on the roof and threw the incendiary bombs off as they fell. I have also heard that at one of Wren's best London churches on that Sunday night, people could see the fires on the roof and would have gone to put them out, but the church was locked and when the key was finally obtained and a way to the roof discovered, the church was past saving. I know that St Paul's has a full complement of watchers who have more than once saved the church from fire. I read that office-blocks are to have fire spotters. Is it not more important that the City churches have fire spotters too? For many years many City churches have hardly been used as places of worship, not for lack of congregation, for the City seethes with people, but for lack of wise use of them. They were used for occasional organ recitals, when the incumbent would run through the liturgy by way of giving a sacred preliminary to the music. For most hours of the week the churches were locked.

There was something grimly ironic about St Vedast's, Foster Lane, when I visited it; the doors were, as usual, locked and the gate in front of them padlocked. But there was no church behind the doors, just an arcade and a heap of rubble to the sky and a smashed font and a brown smoke-streak across the stone steeple. From now on, City churches should be open all day and night and all doors to the roof open and the way to the roof indicated. Yet when I visited the City after the attempt to fire it, many of the surviving churches were as locked as ever, including St Botolph's, Aldersgate, one of the most precious, if one of the latest.

The motto of the City of London is 'Domine dirige nos'. This should encourage its citizens, particularly its vicars and vergers, to preserve its remaining churches, which seem all the more beautiful and restful for the loss of the others.

The fabric of our faith

Punch, 23 December 1953

Lichen-crested granite towers appearing above wind-slashed Cornish elms, smoke coming from the boiler-house chimney on a Saturday afternoon when the stove has been lit for tomorrow's service: noble stone towers and spires in hunting country of the Midlands: huge East Anglian fanes of flint and glass, with angel roofs inside them, old benches, crumbling screens and pale plastered walls: sturdy fortress-like churches of the north: Greek temples in the older industrial towns, and insistent through the roar of the traffic the tinkle from Tudor turrets or Renaissance steeples of bells calling to cedar wood altar pieces: brass chandeliers and ironwork recalling Lord Mayors and Aldermen and civic splendour: red-tiled church roofs of Kent and Sussex which glow like autumn fires above flint and stone walls: no country in the world has such a rich variety of old churches as England.

These buildings are the history of the people of the parish – the humbler under finely carved Georgian headstones, the grander commemorated by masterpieces of eighteenth-century marble in nave and chancel and side chapel. They are the living record, not the museum, of English craftsmanship. And where the Victorians have swept most of the Georgian work away, still enough remains for us to see in the eye of imagination how once the church looked when former generations worshipped in it.

Nor are the Victorians wholly to be condemned. When not restoring but starting from scratch they built some of the noblest churches we possess – St Augustine's, Kilburn; St Stephen's, Bournemouth; St Augustine's, Pendlebury; Hoar Cross, Staffordshire; All Saints', Margaret Street, London; to name only a very few. More lately we have St Peter's, Ealing; St Mary's, Wellingborough; St Cyprian's, Baker Street, London; and Christ Church, Brixton; of which we can be proud.

And the incumbents of our churches are as varied as our buildings: the back-slapping 'padre', pipe-in-mouth and a central churchman: the saintly ascetic whom we call 'Father': the earnest evangelical who calls us 'brother': these good, unworldly men, underpaid, overworked, often the targets of all village rancour, are being diverted from their work of ministering to the sick and feeding the souls of the faithful and converting indifference to belief, by having always to bother about money for the fabric of their churches.

And churches are not the only places of worship which the Historic Churches Trust Fund is to aid. Many beautiful Nonconformist chapels and meeting houses of the seventeenth, eighteenth and early nineteenth centuries, austerely Puritan with clear glass windows, towering pulpits and old high pews, are also in need of repair. To these, too, some of the money will go.

The old churches and chapels of England had been kept in repair by their people's faith and efforts for many centuries. It is the custom today to say no one goes to church and that is why we want so much money – £4,000,000 to help the parishes put their churches into repair. It is not the fault of the Church, which means parsons *and* people, that they are out of repair. People may not go to church today in such numbers as once they did, but those who do go, go because they believe, not because they want to be thought respectable conformers. The bill for church repairs is enormous because during the war years little could be done in the way of small repairs to old churches, the clearing of gutters, the putting back of tiles in a roof or treating a damp patch. There was no one to do the work. By the end of the war, these small repairs had become major ones. When licences could again be obtained, church repairs had to compete for labour and materials with new houses, clinics and community centres and light industry. And money set aside in the war years was totally inadequate to meet the enormous bill for repairs at the inflated prices of the post-war years.

Yet what would England be without her old churches? Not the England we know and love. Too many bishops today, worried by finance and the need for new churches in the growing suburbs and new towns, show a lack of faith by shutting some of them, calling them redundant and selling the sites – often important ones in the heart of a city – in order to find money to build other churches and halls in the new suburbs. They then forget that a church as a building is a more lasting witness to our Christian faith than any bishop, vicar, church-warden or congregation. A civilization is remembered and judged by her buildings. That is why every church, however remote and, maybe only temporarily, unsuccessful, must be kept in repair and open and alive. If we have any faith left, any love of what makes England beautiful and England for us, we will, whatever our version of the Christian faith, subscribe to the Historic Churches Trust until the £4,000,000 has been achieved.

Billy Graham

The Spectator, 12 March 1954

Every night the Harringay arena is packed; every night throngs of converts – mostly young people – crowd up at the end of the service to the bare space below the rostrum, thence to be conducted by 'counsellors' to a room where they are interviewed and given tracts. This is the Greater London Crusade of Billy Graham and I think he must be cynical indeed who affects to despise the crusade or doubt the sincerity of its promoters. If only a tithe of the 'conversions' are lasting, by the end of the campaign the effect on Nonconformity throughout London and the home counties is bound to be enormous. And evangelicals in the Church of England who are now enjoying a revival will also benefit.

Let me say at once that I write as an Anglo-Catholic to whom the revivalistic approach is unattractive. I think it is necessary to be almost indecently lacking in reticence when writing about the Greater London Crusade, for it is not enough just to describe it objectively as though one were looking at an ants' nest and remarking, 'How curious.' I am not shocked by the technique of microphones, massed choirs, trumpets and advertising campaigns. To attract the indifferent today one must, I suppose, shout loudly at first. But I have no memory of a blinding light striking me at the corner of a street, or of a fit of the shudders while people knelt around me in prayer. I cannot point to a date, time and place and say, 'That was when I was converted.' I cling to the sacraments and live for the day, have many moments of doubt when the only thing that buoys me up is the thought that I would sooner the Incarnation were true than that it were not. This, at its lowest ebb, is my faith; but frequent confession and communion have proved to me, unwilling though I sometimes am to believe, that prayer works, that Christ is God, and that He is present in the sacraments of the Church of England. Thus, though I frequently lapse and am rarely exalted, I am conscious of being under divine providence, to use a bit of jargon for which I can think of no clearer substitute, and thankful that I was brought up by Christian parents. For me the growth of faith is gradual and not a sudden revelation. I am sure that Billy Graham himself, who is a Baptist, would be prepared to understand a sacramental approach to Christ. He is not an emotional speaker, despite his wonderful eloquence. It is obviously within his power to make people weep and scream 'Alleluyah'. But he restrains himself. He has the great evangelical love of Our Lord as Man. Jesus as a person is vivid to him. Billy Graham knows his Bible so well, and he brings the scenes of Our Lord's life on earth so vividly before us, that neither catholic nor evangelical could quarrel with him. He is genuinely above religious differences, and if any intolerance or quarrelling comes into the campaign, it will not be Billy Graham's work but the devil's, the product of the protestant underworld of mad sects, or the arrogant uncharity of ultramontanes. The whole burden of his message is that people should return to their particular churches, whether Plymouth Brethren or Church of England. For this reason he holds no services on Sunday in order that people should go back to their own churches.

But what is more impressive than Billy Graham, who is essentially a humble, likeable young man who regards himself merely as an instrument of the Holy Ghost, is the preparation and organization of the Greater London Crusade. For well over a year before it was decided to invite Billy Graham, Nonconformists and evangelical Anglicans engaged in prayer for the conversion of London. He came at the invitation not of one church but of many. And a great many of these 'prayer partners' are in the Harringay arena nightly, and with them 'counsellors', young and old, wearing badges. They have been trained to deal with the stream of converts and to put them in touch with their local churches. I fear that there are few, if any, who are catholics, whether Anglican or Roman, among the 'counsellors'. This is a pity. But those sorts of differences must matter little to people who, as some of the converts are bound to be, don't know who Christ was or what a church or chapel is for. And provided the 'counsellors' have the clarity and breadth of Billy Graham, I do not think we need imagine that their care of converts committed to them will be misdirected.

Sitting in the arena I could pick out easily the earnest, good organizers, prayer partners, stewards and counsellors of the campaign, even if they were not wearing badges to emphasize their identity. I pictured the vast half-empty chapel on some clattering High Road, the sea of pitch-pine pews, and the few people in them leaning forward in their seats and shading their eyes, as the brave disheartened minister asked for God's blessing on Billy Graham and his team. I could see the more crowded interiors of evangelical London churches such as St Peter's, Vere Street, and All Souls', Langham Place, and the young nurses and medical students and clerks, also leaning forward, chapel-wise, and praying as the clergyman read from, I trust, the Book of Common Prayer. And here they all were, at Harringay, with persons whom they had hopes of converting sitting near them.

I foresaw the objectors: the old-fashioned left-wing atheist who sees in it only a plot by American and English businessmen to get the workers to work harder for less money: the smug type, Anglican or Roman, who thinks it all 'dreadfully vulgar and noisy, my dear, and dangerous too, for how are we to protect the apostolic succession?'; the confirmed pessimist who regards it all as a flash in the pan. I foresaw them. But long before I had even heard of the Greater London Crusade, a friend of mine who is an Anglican priest who often visits America said to me: 'A man called Billy Graham is being invited to England. He talks sense, though the way it is put over is not the sort of thing that appeals to you and me. You know: "Are you saved? See Isaiah 44, verses 22 and 23." But it does very well for people less burdened with sophistication than us. I really think that if he has anything like the success he has had in America, when the history of this country comes to be written in a hundred years, Billy Graham's visit will be one of the most important events in it.' We shall see whether that is true.

Meanwhile I think all churches should be grateful for the work which is being done for them. I don't think our own beloved Church of England need fear a landslide yet into it or out of it. People are beginning to think there is something outside what they can touch and see. They are even moving towards the idea of a Creator who cares for us individually. Let the Church go on saying its offices, administering the sacraments, avoiding stunts to fill pews or pandering to the indifference of pampered villagers. Let it not sell all its old churches in the cities to build new ones in the suburbs. In the end the Truth will triumph. And maybe Billy Graham has lessened the time of waiting.

Selling our churches

The Spectator, 2 April 1954

On Easter Sunday the last service will be said in the little church of St Peter, Windmill Street, Piccadilly Circus. The bishop of London has sold the site to a commercial firm for £150,000. One of Prebendary Clarence May's congregation offered the bishop £150,000 to keep the church open. This offer was refused, and we can only conclude that the bishop felt himself so far committed commercially that he would rather sell his church than offend Mammon. I do not know who has bought the site, but if it is to become a restaurant, we may assume that very soon where Londoners worshipped their Saviour on their knees, businessmen will eat meals on their expense accounts.

Beyond some friendly comments on behalf of St Peter's in the London evening papers and the *Church Times*, little publicity has attended the sale. The London Diocesan Advisory Committee, on which I have the honour to sit, was not consulted as to the merits of the building. The congregation, if it was consulted, has resignedly accepted dismissal. The vicar, the Revd Clarence May, has been consoled with a prebendal stall in St Paul's and been told to take his congregation to the far-off church of St George's, Bloomsbury. London churchmen as a whole knew nothing of these negotiations. Much as I admire the bishop of London and his reorganization scheme for the City churches, I know I am not alone in regarding his decision to sell St Peter's, Windmill Street, as short-sighted and unimaginative. For of all sites in Britain, St Peter's is probably today the most valuable mission outpost of the faith now left in the possession of the Church in London.

One reason for its value is that there are so few churches remaining in the West End of London. In the three boroughs of central London, Marylebone, Westminster and Holborn, 47 churches have been demolished since 1904, 4 by German bombs and 43 by bishops. Among recent casualties in the second category we can most of us remember the charming little eighteenth-century parish chapel in Marylebone High Street, which had its box pews, galleries and elegant tablets to parish worthies of Georgian days. It has been pulled down since the war. Many will remember how, travelling on top of a bus down Charing Cross Road, one used to see a great crucifix on the dark red brick east wall of St Mary-the-Virgin's church, with the words under it: 'Is it nothing to you, all ye that pass by?' Apparently it *was* nothing, and that mysterious and imposing interior designed by J. Brookes is gone forever. One of the most beautiful and original churches in London with a cool, grey neo-Romanesque interior was St Anselm's, Davies Street, designed by Balfour and Thackeray Turner. A travesty of it, using some of the stones, has been erected in the northwestern suburbs. But St Andrew's, Wells Street, a far less impressive and mid-Victorian building, was most carefully re-erected in Wembley.

The regret for St Peter's, Windmill Street, can be expressed partly in terms of architecture but mostly in terms of the important position of its site. It is wedged in between Scott's and the Trocadero in that narrow bit of the street which leads from Shaftesbury Avenue to the top of the Haymarket. It is an unobtrusive building in the French Gothic style designed by Raphael Brandon in 1860. Raphael and his brother had designed, five years earlier, the fine Catholic Apostolic church in Gordon Square. Inside, St Peter's has narrow aisles, a lofty nave and apsidal east end. It is dark and homely, the sort of place which the average unin-structed passer-by would think was an old church left behind in London and reminiscent of the village church at home. Moreover, he or she can quickly go into it from the pavement without anyone seeing. Compared with the nearest churches, St Martin-in-the-Fields or St James's, Piccadilly, it is most people's idea of what a church ought to look like. The white and gilded splendour of the Renaissance interiors of these two neighbour-ing churches can never have the same appeal to humble and unsophisti-cated people. As for St Thomas's, Regent Street, the only other church in the crowded heart of London to be left standing, it is often used for plays, with a telephone and ticket office in the porch. And besides that it is yet one more classic building, less splendid than St Martin's or St James's, and so still not a church in the sense in which many people understand that word.

The great value of St Peter's as a mission station is its site. Not a minute passes from 8 a.m. until 1 the next morning without someone passing its locked doors. How many prostitutes or people lost in London, of all ages and races, might not have found sanctuary and advice here, had this church been kept open until midnight and staffed by some organization like the Church Army or Toc H or by a community of mission priests! St Peter's could have been not just a weekday lunch-hour resort, like the

City churches, but one which did well in the evening and late into the night. Then the porch facing the street could have been turned into a bookstall or a church office. As it was, the church was crowded for its Sunday services.

To say that St James's, St Thomas's or St Martin's can supply the need which this perfectly sited little church could have supplied in the most used and depraved part of London is to disregard its geographical situation. It is on an island with a coastline of crowded pavements. Today the rivers of London are not just the Thames but the main roads. To cross the traffic to Piccadilly or to find one's way to Leicester Square is a long and complicated business, more tedious to cross and less inviting than a bridge over the Thames. The lost and bewildered seeking sanctuary would lose heart long before they reached the imposing and comparatively forbidding entrances of St James's or St Martin's.

The argument for the destruction of St Peter's is familiar. 'We want the money to build churches in the vast new suburbs of Greater London.' That may be, but Greater London comes to Piccadilly Circus at all hours of the day. In these days of cheap transport, it is the places where people congregate that also need churches. A live church such as All Saints', Margaret Street, All Souls', Langham Place, or St Martin-in-the-Fields does not have to have residential parishioners to keep it crowded. If it is open and staffed it will attract people who will come from all over London to attend its services. Such a church could St Peter's, Windmill Street, have been. No church in the whole of London was better situated for mission work. It looks to me as though the bishop has been advised by keen young business efficiency experts who, for all their sincerity, have let money and population statistics argue their case for closing the church. But imagination and a little more Faith, Hope and Charity would have kept it open.

The spirit of Christmas

Housewife, December 1954

Christmas is for many of us a long succession of Sundays when we run out of cigarettes and are not able to buy any till next Tuesday and today's only Friday; the day after Christmas Day means a slight attack of liver through drinking a sticky and horrible liqueur on Christmas Day which one of our children gave us, but which we secretly think was hair oil and didn't like to say so for fear of giving offence; the Bank Holiday after Christmas (and we are in for rather more days off than usual this year) means infinitely frayed tempers at home through lack of exercise. The end of the Christmas holiday comes as a return to the drudgery of the office, with the trains rather unnecessarily full because of all the people who have been away with their relations.

In this jaundiced mood all things to do with Christmas become suspect. Most intolerable is the racket of Christmas cards. There are varieties of horror, quite apart from the designs: there are those which are frankly commercial from tradesmen, which only serve to remind us of unpaid bills; there are facetious ones disguised to advertise the personality of the sender, a forgotten acquaintance and not a friend, and expecting a reply because the address is given in full; there are those with an indecipherable signature – perhaps it is someone we know well who will be bitterly offended at not hearing from us this Christmas. There are tremendously expensive Christmas cards from people who have made a sacrifice to send them to us and we know that the one we sent them is much cheaper and will be noticed as such. And, of course, there are those who have sent us Christmas cards and to whom we have forgotten to send one in return.

On Boxing Day we go to the home of friends and see that they have had more Christmas cards than we have had. Feeling touchy and embarrassed, we cast surreptitious glances at their display of cards along shelves, on the piano and even above the pelmet of their curtains. We wonder why so-and-so bothered to send them a Christmas card and not one to us. We also notice that the one the taxi-hire service sent them is much more handsome and expensive than the one they sent to us.

This is the place to give some advice about dealing with Christmas cards. The old trick of leaving the '6d' price on and with faint pencil strokes turning it into '1/6d' is now played out. I advise the bold line taken by a friend of mine, Mrs Eustace Cadgwith. When she received a printed card saying 'Wishing you and yours a happy Christmas, from the Anglo-Persian Petroleum Company,' she used to add 'and Mr and Mrs Eustace Cadgwith' and post it on to someone else.

Rather incensed by commercial companies cashing in on the Christian festival of Christmas, I had a lot of cards printed with the single word ETERNITY in huge capital letters. I sent this to all commercial firms which sent me Christmas cards. I have had none since from those sources. I also sent it to Communist friends. It has always surprised me how ardent unbelievers, to whom the birth of Christ is an exploded piece of folklore, are most assiduous in sending out Christmas cards.

Hitherto I have been writing of Christmas in the spirit of Scrooge and not of Christmas. At the risk of sounding like a clergyman, let me suggest that the only way to weather Christmas is to treat it for what it is, a time of thanksgiving for our salvation. Christmas is the celebration of the birth of Christ.

If the Christian religion is true, and most of us call ourselves Christians and therefore tend to think it is true, then the only really important event in all history is when the Creator of the stars, this world, the sky, you and me and the materials which we rely on to sustain life and entertain ourselves, the Maker of the men who made the paper on which this is printed, Who made the ink-makers and the printers and our brains, and insects and animals and trees and hills and sea, in fact, the Creator of us all, became Man and was born in Bethlehem nearly 2,000 years ago. On that day Eternity came humbly into time and put on human flesh and was a Baby in the stable of an inn. If that is true, then to that great day all the earlier history and pre-history of the world was leading; towards that day all subsequent history looks back, which is why we know this as the one thousand and nine hundred and fifty-fourth year from the birth of Christ.

It is not difficult to understand, but it is very difficult to believe. Personally, I find the only way I can accept this truth is by receiving Holy Communion in the form of bread and wine and not inquiring too deeply into how this is food for my soul, but just accepting it in good faith and with as clear a conscience as possible. Often it seems to me quite improbable. But if it isn't true, I can see no point in anything and I would rather it were true. If it is true it gives point to everything, and Christmas is the greatest birthday in the year, and no presents we give and no kindnesses we show each other at Christmas can adequately express our thanksgiving.

Therefore on Christmas Day I will do as the Book of Common Prayer of the Church of England enjoins me, and go to Holy Communion in the morning. Christmas Eve will have been a solemn time of waiting and Christmas Day will be a day of rejoicing and eating, and giving presents, and hearing church bells, and wearing, with as cheerful a countenance as possible, the violent new tie I received as a present from one of the less critical but more affectionate members of my household. In this spirit, the long succession of Sundays, which Christmas seems, will be a happy rest. There is no doubt that people are pleasanter at Christmas, just as they are when the sun shines. There is a feeling of rejoicing in the air.

Now let me take another look at those Christmas cards. There are among them several which were sent out of pure goodness of heart by poor people to whom the stamp and the card represented a sacrifice. These are the cards really worth receiving; they justify the Christmas card habit and cancel out the commercialism of Christmas. And in this exalted mood, I can even look with tolerance on the cards which are nothing but advertisements. At least there is no harm in them. And how delightful it is, when one goes out, to find those who are usually sour passing the time of day with one.

The best thing of all about Christmas, once one has got oneself into this mood of thanksgiving, is the chance it gives for uniting families before it is too late and all one's relations have died. For the saddest of all Christmases are those spent in hotels by old people whose relations have forgotten them. I see in my mind's eye the little bedroom of the aged permanent resident; I see the three or four cards, one from a nephew in Kenya, another from a distant daughter-in-law, a third from the hotel management, and the last from a school-friend now bedridden. I visualize this aged resident saving half-crowns from her diminished annuity to give as a tip to the maid who has a family of her own to go back to and who will be off duty on Christmas Day. I see this aged resident go down the stairs to the feebly decorated lounge of the hotel. There will be Christmas dinner in the hotel today: not very good turkey and a hard, dry slice of Christmas pudding. There will be only three or four other lost and forgotten people staying, and perhaps some foreigners to whom Christmas is not the great feast it is in England. No relation is too tiresome and too old, at any rate, to be asked to come home for Christmas, even if in one's heart of hearts one hopes she will refuse to come. Nor need blood have to be the only tie for asking these lonely people.

I have been told, and experience has proved it, too, that English people are some of the kindest in the world. I daresay that this kindness springs from their goodwill which always receives a new impetus at the great Christian festival of Christmas.

The Church Union as Defender of the Faith

Church Times, 27 June 1958

There must be many who remember the great days of the Anglo-Catholic Congress in the 'twenties – the vestments, the birettas, the clouds of incense and, below all the surface colour and excitement, the firm assertion of our faith:

> And then, by men and angels
> Thy name shall be adored,
> And this shall be their anthem
> One Church, One Faith, One Lord.
> E. H. Plumptre, 1821–91

Young divines with pale ascetic faces who carried banners then, swarthy Rugger toughs who swung the incense, are now, maybe, the greying incumbents of suburban parishes or far away in the mission field. Some may even be bishops. The Anglo-Catholic Congress amalgamated with the old established English Church Union and reappeared under the title of the Church Union. It is this combined body which celebrates its centenary this year, most appropriately, with a Eucharistic Congress.

On 12 May 1859 the Church of England Protection Society was formed to protect the rights of priests and worshippers which in those days were being threatened by the State, heavily backed by Queen Victoria, acting through secular courts on Church matters. In the next year the society changed its name to the English Church Union, and in April 1868 the Hon. Charles Lindley Wood, who became Lord Halifax in 1885, was elected its president, an office which he held with authority, tact, balance, courage and distinction until his retirement in 1919 on grounds of health. But he returned as president a few years later and continued in office until his death in 1934. The objects of the Church of England Protection Society were: (1) to defend and maintain unimpaired the doctrine and discipline of the Church of England; (2) in general, so to promote the interests of religion as to be, by God's help, a lasting witness in the land for the advancement of the glory and the good of his Church; (3) to afford counsel and protection to all persons, lay or clerical, suffering under unjust aggression or hindrance in spiritual matters. Those are still the objects today. The Church of England is catholic and reformed. People are inclined to forget that it is catholic in their enthusiasm for reform. That is why the Church Union has to exist. But its history goes back centuries before 1859.

Before the publication of Dr Cross's admirable *Oxford Dictionary of the Christian Church*, many of us had recourse to Dr J. H. Blunt's late-Victorian *Dictionary of Sects, Theories, and Ecclesiastical Parties*, which was written from a vigorously Anglican point of view, certain that the Church of England is of apostolic origin, and distinctly 'High Church' in its tone. Dr Blunt, in his article on 'High Churchmen', gives a clear account which may be summarized thus. The High Churchmen of the Reformation age (Bishop Ridley and the prayer book divines, Archbishops Parker and Bancroft, Hooper) saved the Church from becoming Lutheranized or Calvinized by preserving its continuity with the English Church of preceding ages. The High Churchmen of the seventeenth century (Bishop Andrewes, Bishop Hubert, Archbishop Laud, Bishop Cosin, Archbishop Sancroft and the Non-Jurors) restored health to the Church when it was being destroyed by Presbyterianism. The High Churchmen of the eighteenth century (Nelson, South, Dean Stanhope, Bishop Butler, Bishop Gibson, Archbishop Wake, Dr Johnson, Wilkins, Wheatley) withstood the dangers of that scepticism which overturned the Church of France. Those of the early nineteenth century (Bishop Jebb, Alex Knox, Dr Routh, Bishop Van Mildert, Archbishop Howley, Bishop Phillpotts) revived ecclesiastical learning and through the influence of the Tractarians (Newman, Pusey, Keble, Isaac Williams) carried the influence of the Church home to the hearts of rich and poor in face of difficulties arising from very novel conditions of social, religious and intellectual life.

The English Church Union continued the work of these men. In the 'sixties, the outward expression of the faith of the Church was shown by 'Ritualists' who, by lighting two candles on the altar, taking the Eastward position, using wafers and vestments, be the latter only a coloured stole, roused a Protestant fury. People then thought, as some still do, that any outward assertion of the catholic faith in the way of colour and action is tantamount to being a Roman Catholic. The ECU defended the Ritualists. It defended the faith of the Church when Archdeacon Denison and later Mr Bennett of Frome were attacked for teaching the accepted doctrine of the Church of England on the Real Presence. In 1874, when the Public Worship Regulation Act was passed and five priests were imprisoned by civil courts for teaching the catholic faith in their churches, it supported them in all their sufferings. In the 'eighties the 'Modernist' attacks started. Here the ECU went into aggressive action, having hitherto been on the defence. More recently, when Bishop Barnes boycotted a number of his priests working in the poorest parts of Birmingham, it gave them grants to continue their witness and work.

The ECU always sought to preserve the catholic faith in the Church. In the conversations Lord Halifax and various ECU members had in Rome in 1894 and with Cardinal Mercier in 1920 on the subject of reunion, there was not any suggestion on either side of the Anglican Church denying its apostolic origin, but of arranging some understanding between the Roman Catholics and ourselves, whereby the unfortunate duplication of catholic teaching which goes on in England today could be avoided. This, it seems, is not yet to be.

I hope I will be forgiven for introducing a personal note, for it has some bearing on the work of the Church Union. I was baptized in the Church of England as a baby, but had not accepted the full catholic faith until I was an undergraduate at Oxford, where I was instructed at Pusey House. Since then I have never doubted the Presence of our Lord in the Blessed Sacrament, nor the validity of absolutions I have received after my confessions. If I worship in an Anglican church where the clergyman takes the Northward position for Holy Communion, it has always occurred to me that whatever *he* may think about the service of Holy Communion, himself, it is still the same Communion as that at All Saints', Margaret Street, or St Magnus the Martyr, London Bridge. And when I die I hope that I may be buried by the last rites of the Church in which I was born.

Of course there are times, as there probably are for many of us, when I think the Christian religion is not true, and there are other times when I wish that it were not true, for it is often inconvenient and restrictive on delightful indulgencies to which I am prone. But at least I can thank God that I have never thought the Church of England had not the full catholic faith, all seven sacraments, and was not of God. And if I were inclined to doubt its validity, I would only have to look out of my window, here in Wantage where I write, at St Michael's House opposite me, where live those Wantage Sisters who have grown old in the faith; I have only to think of the hundreds of fine Victorian churches rising out of the slums, of our missionaries all over the world, and then to ask myself, have all these people been deluded? More learned and far cleverer people than I have thought not. Of course our Church is the Catholic Church in England. If it had not been so, it would have died out long ago.

It is to the Church Union and its predecessors that we are indebted for the upholding of its catholic doctrine and discipline by instruction, by negotiation, by literature and word of mouth. Next week, at the Eucharistic Congress at the Albert Hall, 'The World for God', it will be doing so again. I pray that the old impetus of the Catholic Church's revival of the 'twenties will return.

> Our fathers owned thy Goodness,
> And we their deeds record;
> And both of this bear witness,
> One Church, One Faith, One Lord.
> E. H. Plumptre, 1821–91

A passion for churches

BBC2 Television, 7 December 1974

I was eight or nine years old when I used to come here to the Norfolk Broads on the River Bure, sailing and rowing with my father. And I think it was the outline of that church tower of Belaugh against the sky that gave me a passion for churches, so that every church I've been past since I've wanted to stop and look in.

The air: the Old Hundredth. The place: Bressingham. The diocese: Norwich, which includes most of Norfolk and a little bit of Suffolk.

> What would you be, you wide East Anglian sky,
> Without church towers to recognize you by?
> What centuries of faith, in flint and stone,
> Wait in this watery landscape, all alone?
> To antiquaries, 'object of research';
> To the bored tourist, 'just another church'.
> The varied Norfolk towers could also be
> A soothing sight to mariners at sea.

This is Cley-next-the-Sea. The sea is now quite a long way off. It's a tiny place but it's got an enormous church. They must have had hopes of it being very much bigger. And look at that porch – built, I should think, about 1430. Very delicately done: almost another church in itself; and slapped onto it, very coarsely, a sundial. Time suddenly stuck into eternity.

Look at that, for vastness and light: light falling on carved Norfolk oak, gone silvery-grey with age. And towards the light come out the nightmare figures of marsh and forest: earth-bound creatures struggling up the bench-ends. They know they can never reach the winged celestial hosts here in the roof at Knapton.

The finest of all the woodcarving is in the neighbouring parish of Trunch. It exalts the very first sacrament: baptism by water – the first armour we put on against the assaults of hate, greed and fear on our journey back to eternity. 'Cherry Ann: your godparents make promises on your behalf and the village of Trunch bears witness.'

First steps on the journey. At Mattishall they have Sunday school on Wednesday afternoon. The 'Little People', as they call them, clutching their tambourines and triangles, come to hear the old story told anew.

Each generation makes itself heard. The past cries out to us even when we try to smother the cries. Medieval saints peer at us through godly warnings put over them by pious Elizabethans who had more use for the written word than the painted picture. We can help the past come through a hundredth of an inch at a time. Miss Pauline Plummer is revealing the secrets of the chancel screen at Ranworth and soon will show it in its medieval glory.

In the fifteenth century Norwich was famous for its painters. They delighted in herbs and flowers and living creatures. The lithe and feathered figure of the Archangel Michael is by no provincial hand. It's rather a masterpiece. The Norwich artists also painted on glass, and light came in to every Norfolk church through golden late-medieval windows.

Men hate beauty. They think it's wicked. Self-righteous churchwardens delighted in smashing it. Village boys flung stones. Storms did the rest. Today the famous Norwich glass is nearly all jumbled fragments. A few whole windows survive.

Here's where the artists worked: the city of Norwich, down in the valley of the Wensum. It's a city of cobbled alleys and winding footpaths. It has more medieval churches within its walls than London, York and Bristol put together. Remember Norwich. Round the corner, down the steps, over the bridge, up the hill – there's always a church. And grandest of all, St Peter Mancroft – so large that sometimes people mistake it for the cathedral.

The city wears its cathedral like a crown: a coronal of flying buttresses supporting the walls of glass. The Normans started it. The stone was brought over the sea from France to build and adorn the Cathedral Church of the Holy and Undivided Trinity. It draws the whole diocese towards it; and in its cloisters, made for contemplation, mothers and grandmothers, vicars and rectors from the towns and villages of the diocese of Norwich gather together for the annual festival of the Mothers' Union.

Bawdeswell greets Stratton Strawless. Potter Heigham is on terms with Little Snoring. North Creake sits beside Melton Constable. And for everyone there's the chance to meet the bishop: Maurice Wood, Diocesan Bishop of Norwich. When not entertaining, he's Maurice Norvic, Father-in-God to the clergy.

The bishop institutes a new rector to the living of Holt in north Norfolk. By the laying on of hands, the bishop commits to the priest the spiritual care of the parish.

With every parish church there's a house, rectory or vicarage – usually beside the churchyard. I think you probably need money of your own to be rector of Great Snoring because the rectory house is a Tudor palace, with moulded autumn-coloured brick and elaborate chimney stacks. And the date: about 1525. It's the usual practice now, though, to sell big rectories and build labour-saving villas in their place.

At Weston Longville, in Georgian days, Parson Woodforde wrote his worldly diaries, full of good dinners. The present rector types the parish magazine. Reverend James:

> We send belated birthday greetings to Mr Walter Pardon of Weston Longville who reached the splendid age of 89 years on February 17th.
> Little Johnny Atherton, aged three-and-a-half years, broke his leg on February 17th. Bad luck. We hope you get well soon, Johnny.
> It is only a rumour but there is talk of a sponsored streak for church funds.

By whom? we wonder. Not, I think, by members of the Parochial Church Council at Letheringsett: the PCC. It's meeting this evening in the church hall, with the rector in the chair.

If it isn't the tower, it's the transept or the north porch. And the answer is usually a fête to raise another few pounds. We can rely on the parish to rally round.

> God bless the Church of England,
> The rectory lawn that gave
> A trodden space for that bazaar
> That underpinned the nave.
> We must dip into our pockets,
> For our hearts are full of dread
> At the thought of all the damage
> Since the roof was stripped of lead.

And it's always worth a try to get the key, however remote the church. In fact, the remoter the better: there's more chance of its being left unspoiled.

St Mary's Bylaugh, in the valley of the Wensum. Look. The pulpit. This is a perfect example of a church in a park in the time of Jane Austen. The woodwork is all of oak. Notice that altarpiece with the Creed, the Commandments and the Lord's Prayer painted on it, and here is a three-decker pulpit in full sail. This is where the parish clerk said 'Amen' at the end of the prayers and announced the name of the hymn tune or the psalm tune. Here, a gentle staircase leads to the middle deck and this is where the minister, as he was called, read the holy offices of Morning and Evening Prayer and the lessons. And if he was in the mood, or if it was the fourth Sunday in the month or something like that, he would ascend to the top deck to preach a sermon. And from here the parson could survey his whole parish. In the big box pew there, the squire from the hall, slumbering while a fire crackled in the grate; the large farmers in the pews in front; the cottagers and lesser tenantry behind; all by country custom in their place in the church by law established.

The cottagers and lesser tenantry would have had a good long walk by field and footpath to the isolated parish church of St Margaret, Felbrigg. The squire would have had a gentle stroll: it is in the park of the big house. I wonder who fall to their knees here today?

Oh – the new cottage industry: brass-rubbing. Memorial brasses to former generations of squires of Felbrigg and their ladies. Medieval effigies that tell us nothing of the people they represent, they're so calm and bland and self-controlled. Outlined there, as large as life, Sir Simon and Lady Margaret Felbrigg: he a Garter knight and she a cousin of the Queen. It must have been the day of days, the day they took their vows.

Ringing the changes, treble bell to tenor, unites young and old. Captain of the Tower and 60 years a ringer, Billy West:

BILLY WEST: Ah, that's music in your ear, that's music in the ear. Once that gets hold of you, I suppose that's like smoking cigarettes; once that gets a hold of you that, that's a drug: you can't get rid of it. There's something about it, I don't know what it is, but you'd go anywhere for it. If there weren't somewhere where there were some bells I'd go crazy, I know I should. Bells are life to me. I mean, it never seems a Sunday to me if we don't hear the bells. That never seems Sunday if you can't hear church bells going.

BETJEMAN:

> I hear a deep, sad undertone in bells –
> Which calls the Middle Ages back to me.
> From prime to compline, the monastic hours
> Echo in bells along the windy marsh
> And fade away. They leave me to the ghosts
> Which seem to look from this enormous sky
> Upon the ruins of a grandeur gone.
> St Benet's Abbey by the River Bure:

Now but an archway and a Georgian mill –
A lone memorial of the cloistered life.
Alone? No, not alone. Serene, secure,
The sisters of All Hallows, Ditchingham,
In this brick convent, for over a century now,
Have taught and trained the young and nursed the sick
And founded rescue homes.
A homely practical community.
Their souls are fed with daily Eucharists.
You see the impress there upon the bread;
You see the impress also in their lives.
Their motto:
Semper orantes, semper laborantes.
Always at prayer, and always at their work.
An Anglican convent in East Anglia.
A place to think of when the world seems mad
With too much speed and noise.
A pleasant place to come to for retreat.
There's really not much risk of being stung. [The scene
    reveals bee-keeping]

Just as some people are holy, so are places. They draw us to them whether
we will or not. In the misty past in the 1920s and '30s people came to Norfolk by train, by steam: by the Great Eastern and more locally by the Mid-
and and Great Northern Joint. They came on pilgrimage by train, faith-
enlightened, full of hope and on the way to Walsingham. This is all that
remains of the railway track that carried all those pilgrims to Walsingham.

And what's become of the station? It's the Orthodox church. The Orient
come to East Anglia, to this country town, where in 1061 (forgive my
mentioning dates) the Lady of the Manor saw the Virgin Mary, Mother
of God.

> Then medieval pilgrims, peasants, kings,
>   In thousands thronged to England's Nazareth.

The cult has been revived in modern times; suburbanized, perhaps. The
Shrine of Our Lady of Walsingham: 1930s red-brick Romanesque. But
inside is the goal of all the pilgrims. And very peculiar it is.

> I wonder if you'd call it superstitious?
> Here in this warm, mysterious, holy house,
> The figure of Our Lady and Her Child;

> Or do you think that forces are around,
> Strong, frightening, loving and just out of reach
> But waiting, waiting, somewhere to be asked?
> And is that somewhere here at Walsingham?
> The water bubbles from the Holy Well.
> By water we were brought into the Church;
> By water we are blessed along the way.

I've seen processions like this in Sicily. You can see them in the streets of Malta, too. But it's an exotic flowering of the Church of England, here in a Norfolk garden. The Anglican Church has got a bit of everything. It's very tolerant – and that is part of its strength.

Farewell to the pilgrims; here come the tourists. Sandringham is the Queen's country estate. The parish church is used by both the villagers and the royal family. It seems appropriate to arrive in style. [Betjeman is shown arriving in an old Bentley.]

Originally, says the guidebook, Sandringham church had little or nothing to distinguish it from any village church in Norfolk. Well, at first glance it rather reminds me of the Wee Kirk o' the Heather in Hollywood: those silver panels on the pulpit, that jewel-encrusted Bible. But in fact it's very Edwardian, for here worshipped King Edward VII and Queen Alexandra. The ornate furnishings, this altar of solid silver, were given by Mr Rodman Wanamaker, a very rich American admirer of our royalty.

Sandringham church has its homely touches, too. Of all the details in this church I think this is my favourite. You can tell from the swirls and the curves who the sculptor was. He was Sir Alfred Gilbert, who designed, you'll remember, Eros in Piccadilly Circus. In Sandringham he's done the figure of St George.

> I wade my way alone, no tourists near,
> Through last year's autumn leaves
> To Booton's haunting weird Victorian church.
> Its pinnacles outlined against the sky
> Seem outsize pinnacles, copies of others elsewhere,
> But they look so big
> I fear the church will topple with their weight.
> A rich Victorian rector paid for them
> And paid for all the stained-glass windows too.
> No painful crucifixions here.
> The heavenly choir, in Victorian dress,
> Makes joyful music unto the Lord of Hosts.

Let everything that hath breath praise the Lord – but practise first in the rectory at Martham, between the Broads and the sea. (Meanwhile, in his room above, the rector, Father Cooling, model engineer, oils his parish wheels [the rector is busy with his model trains] – and indeed they run themselves most smoothly.) Everywhere church choirs prepare for Easter. Wymondham's Norman abbey is the town's parish church; and in this century Sir Ninian Comper made the east wall a lofty reredos of sculptured gold. Scale is the secret of its majesty.

Scale was Comper's secret. In 1914 they let him loose in this plain old country church. He turned it into a treasure house. The golden church of Lound, Suffolk, in the diocese of Norwich. Gold on the font cover to emphasize the sacrament of Baptism – entry into the Church; gold on the screen to veil the mystery of Holy Communion at the high altar.

I knew Comper. He died a few years ago and he looked rather like that advertisement for Colonel Sanders Kentucky chicken. Little white pointed beard and he spoke in a very lah-di-dah manner: 'My wark, doncha know, in that charch . . .' And his wark in this charch is really marvellous. I think this is what a late-medieval English church probably looked like when it was new. Colour very important; saints, angels and symbolic figures everywhere. Comper was much influenced by the colour and decoration of Spanish, Sicilian and Greek churches. He didn't mind about style. Sometimes he mixed Classical with Gothic. That he called 'unity by inclusion'.

As I look through this rood screen I can see the colours of the altar hangings. Pink predominates. It's called Comper Pink, and he had it specially made in Spain. He used to buy scarlet silk and there have it bleached in the sun till it was just the shade he wanted. 'Incomperable', as people used to say. 'A church should pray of itself with its architecture,' said Comper. 'It is its own prayer and should bring you to your knees when you come in.'

But there's another way. At his ordination, every Anglican priest promises to say Morning and Evening Prayer, daily. The vicar of Flordon has rung the bell for Matins each day for the past 11 years. It doesn't matter that there's no one there. It doesn't matter when they do not come. The villagers know the parson is praying for them in their church.

> In some churches all prayer has ceased.
> St Benedict's, Norwich, is a tower alone.
> But better let it stand
> A lighthouse beckoning to a changing world.
> St Edmund Fishergate – a store for soles of shoes.

> Once it was working for the souls of men.
> Churches are what make Norwich different.
> 'A church for every Sunday of the year,'
> They used to say of it. 'A use for every church'
> Is what we say today. St Lawrence here –
> Spacious and filled with mitigated light.
> The matchless words of the Book of Common Prayer
> Once rolled along these walls.
> Now young artists use it for a studio.
> Better that than let the building fall.

Artists come to St Mary Coslany, too. In this church John Sell Cotman, the Norfolk watercolour painter, was baptized, and here Crome the artist was married. The present congregation is well upholstered. It is all stored here for charity.

> A use for every church – a thought not new.
> Four hundred years ago St Helen's, Norwich,
> Became a hostel and a hospital.
> Men in the nave, ladies in the chancel,
> The parish church in between.
> This is the upper floor of the chancel, the Eagle Ward.
> And here you can be cared for till you die.
> And should we let the poor old churches die?
> Do the stones speak? My word, of course they do.
> Here in the midst of life they cry aloud:
> 'You've used us to build houses for your prayer;
> You've left us here to die beside the road.'
> Christ, son of God, come down to me and save:
> How fearful and how final seems the grave.
> Only through death can resurrection come;
> Only from shadows can we see the light;
> Only at our lowest comes the gleam:
> Help us, we're all alone and full of fear.
> Drowning, we stretch our hands to you for aid
> And wholly unexpectedly you come:
> Most tolerant and all-embracing Church.

Wide is the compass of the Church of England. The Smith's Point lighthouse is the furthest point of the Norwich diocese, 22 miles out to sea. The Revd Maurice Chant, Chaplain of the Missions to Seamen in Great

Yarmouth, comes aboard to meet the men, see if there are any problems and to be there just in case he's needed. He distributes the Mission's magazine and pastoral greetings.

On inland waters, Canon Blackburne, Chaplain of the Norfolk Broads, summons the floating members of his flock to Easter service.

Easter Day. Dawn over the easternmost tip of Britain: Ness Point, Lowestoft. At six o'clock in the morning, led by the band of the Salvation Army, all churches join in the first Easter service and greet the rising sun.

> Peaceful their Lives are, calm and unsurprising,
> The almshouse ladies here at Castle Rising;
> And suited to the little brick-built square
> The Jacobean hats and cloaks they wear.
> See from the separate rooms in which they dwell
> Each one process. The Warden pulls the bell:
> Fingers and knees not yet too stiff to pray
> And thank the Lord for life this Easter Day.
> Bells of St Peter Mancroft loudly pealing
> Fill the whole city with an Easter feeling.
> 'Is risen today, is risen today,' they plead,
> Where footpath, lane and steep up-alley lead.
> Across the diocese from tower to tower
> The church bells exercise compelling power.
> 'Come all to church, good people,' hear them say;
> 'Come all to church, today is Easter Day.'
> Over our vicar we may not agree,
> He seems too High to you, too Low to me;
> But still the faith of centuries is seen
> In those who walk to church across the green.
> The faith of centuries is in the sound
> Of Easter bells that ring all Norfolk round;
> And though for church we may not seem to care,
> It's deeply part of us. Thank God it's there.

Part 2

CHRISTIAN AESTHETICS

'There is no doubt that you have transformed church architecture in England and you stand on your own as the only creative genius in that sphere. . . . I wonder how many hundreds have been instructed in Catholicism by your planning, delicacy of proportion, texture and colour? Many, I suspect – me for one. . . . So long as you go on doing what only you in England can do, you will be doing God's will.'

Letter to Ninian Comper, 12 October 1939

1837–1937: A spiritual change is the one hope for art

The Studio, February 1937

The drift towards ugliness

The history of the last hundred years of taste in England is profoundly influenced by three things: increase in population, mass production, absence of any uniting faith. The development of Boggleton, a small English town which I have traced at set periods in the next pages, is symptomatic of all England. We can learn the character of the country from the scars and wrinkles on its face. Probably no other place in Europe was so beautiful as England in 1820, few are uglier than it is round its larger towns today. In 1820 there were high standards of craftsmanship and certain canons of taste. Today craftsmanship has gone, or is revived, without any appreciable influence, by escapists. Canons of taste are as uncertain as they are various. The history of Boggleton may help to show how this has come about, and for those who prefer their art history in terms of generalizations I have summarized each section with some general remarks.

1837

It is interesting to analyse, as one enters an English provincial town today, the statement that no error of taste was committed before 1340 and to consider how far it is true. A provincial town presents a complete history of nineteenth-century taste which is still traceable underneath the hoardings, neon signs and wires with which progress has strung every feature of urban and even rural landscape. And there is no doubt that architecture is the outward and visible form of inward and spiritual grace or disgrace. So it is with architecture I propose to start this account.

The topographical dictionary (1837) describes Boggleton as a neat market-town standing in an elevated position on the slopes of the Bogdown hills. The subsoil is limestone. The population is 3,000. The chief industries are flint knapping, for flint-lock muskets, and agriculture. There is a decent town hall recently erected (1825); an ancient parish church situated not far from the centre of the town, an independent chapel and a meeting house for the Society of Friends in Bowling Green Alley. Magnificent views are obtainable from the common, a considerable expanse to the south to which freeholders have had the right of free pasturage since the time of King John.

And what the topographical dictionary omits, the eye of the traveller will discern as he bowls through the main street in his coach and four, putting up at The Dolphin where there is adequate stabling for his horses. The main street of Boggleton is of even appearance. It is wide and well-proportioned and the Doric columns of the new town hall make a fine termination to the vista which the traveller sees as he approaches from London.

On either side of the town hall are the more considerable shops, each with square-paned windows and a uniform style of lettering above them in gold. Plain Georgian houses rise above the shop fronts, the windows on the first floor being larger than those on the second and those on the second being larger than those on the top. The roofs are hidden by a low parapet. The material of the houses is mostly limestone, but the town hall and The Dolphin, which are larger than any other buildings in the street, are of white brick from the recently opened brick-fields outside the town. They are plain but imposing edifices whose beauty depends on that subtlety of proportion which all architects of the late Georgian era had learned from the close study of Greek art and its adaptation to modern buildings, as expressed in the lectures of Sir John Soane. Breaking the uniform grey of these substantial buildings in limestone and plaster or white brick is a large, mellow red-brick mansion, the thick white glazing bars of whose windows, the subtle classical stone-carving of whose keystones, cornices and dressings, the heavy solidity of whose panelled front door, coupled with the absence of any sign of commerce in the way of shop front or sign, betrays the presence of some wealthy person of private means. This is Adamsbec House, the town residence of the Adamsbecs, whose large country estate and house is some distance away. The family rarely comes to it now since the improved method of highway travel has brought the metropolis within nearer reach. Except for this cluster of buildings round the centre of the town, Boggleton will not present much of architectural interest to the traveller of 1837.

The rest of the High Street diminishes London-wards into what are little more than stone cottages, some of them bulging with bow-windowed shop fronts or standing apart to admit a glimpse of the meadows to the south and the elm-clad hills to the north of the town. Down one of these alleys is the Quaker meeting house, a simple affair in limestone with scrubbed benches and white walls within and nicely graded tiled roof distinguishing its plain exterior. The independent chapel is also a plain building (1794) resembling, with its two storeys of round-headed windows, a thin private house. It is a little more obtrusive than the Quaker meeting house, since it was put up after the persecution of Nonconformists and dares to show itself in the High Street.

The ancient parish church will attract the traveller's antiquarian but not his aesthetic attention. It is an irregular building in the late pointed style. It stands a little distance behind the town hall and is surrounded by alleys between cottages, some of which are built of clunch and clearly very ancient, though scarcely genteel. The church, indeed, stands in the old centre of the town and the cottages round it are a survival, built in the haphazard medieval way of growing, of the village which Boggleton was before it became an agricultural centre, for Boggleton was never a planned medieval city within walls. The citizens objected to their common being used for sales, so a site north of the church was used for bargaining, where the road entered the village. This was built round and gradually became the market place and new centre of Boggleton life.

The interior of the parish church presents a venerable appearance. An elaborately carved wooden screen runs across the chancel and north chapel. The walls are whitewashed and form a handsome gallery of hatchments and mural monuments. Some of the latter were done by a talented stonemason in the town from a book of engravings for mural monuments published by I. Taylor in 1787. The pews are of good deal and comfortable, being of excellent joinery with well-fitting doors. The cushions in them are of watered silk and one pew at least has a stove in it which warms Mr Awdon and his family, merchant and mayor of the town. There is a west gallery for the choir whose instruments are kept there out of the way of the ringers below. The three-decker pulpit is used by the now ageing incumbent who celebrates quarterly Communion.

Having inspected the church and refreshed himself, the coachman and horses, the traveller will pass on towards Adamsbecton, the large country house of the Adamsbec family. About a mile out of the town, the ruins of Godley Abbey rise up among the willows and elms of the valley. The pile is a monument to superstition, but at the same time it has much of the sublime, seeming to draw towards it the surrounding hills.

A row of genteel houses looks on the abbey from the further side of the road. These are airy and cheerful, having been built in 1820. They are in a variety of styles. One is Grecian with a wide verandah commanding the prospect: the other is something like it but plainer and of three storeys with a balcony of elegant ironwork on the first floor. The third is called the Oratory and is in the Gothic taste with pointed windows and an octagonal parlour, a veritable monkish cell. This is nearer the abbey than the other two houses, and is calculated to blend in with that structure. The houses are inhabited by a retired merchant, a retired naval captain, the younger son of a family whose fortunes have declined, and two maiden ladies, daughters of a former rector of Boggleton.

Our traveller will now have little to attract him after this glimpse of the picturesque until he comes to Adamsbecton. There he will be permitted to see the gallery which contains a Salvator Rosa, a Lawrence, a Reynolds, three Lelys, a Murillo, a Canaletto and a Guido Reni, as well as several paintings of the Dutch school and even more of the Italian schools.

The people of Boggleton take their town for granted, just as our traveller takes the hospitality of Adamsbecton for granted. Carpenters, masons and builders are good craftsmen and an architect building in the district can rely on them to do their work well and supply the appropriate mouldings in the specified places. Merchants are unhampered by undue rivalry and the farmers are prosperous. The gentry are, many of them, liberal. Only the meaner sort have cause for complaint.

The last days of tradition

The most significant thing about the arts of this time was not the usual clash between classic and romantic, but the tradition of craftsmanship which pervaded everything from the mouldings round the lintel of a door to the title page of a book.

The machine was getting into its stride, but the British tradition of thoroughness had not yet died out. The knowledge of detail inherited from a system of apprenticeship appears in the exquisite bindings of books, the high standard of engraving, the chaste layout of the typographer. No work was skimped. Even the speculative builder had a civic conscience and laid out several stuccoed estates round our larger towns which for spaciousness of planning and aesthetic beauty have yet to be improved upon in our own era of town-planning.

The classic and romantic clash must certainly be considered. The classic comes first and there is no doubt that its greatest exponent was Sir John Soane, who invented a severe style of architecture which is the envy of every European country except its own. Artists of all sorts still went on the Grand Tour and those who could not afford it made careful drawings of classical sculpture, notably the Elgin marbles. There were certain dogmatic rules laid down for art. Traditional forms and compositions pervaded everything. Art criticism was, mercifully, in its infancy and had not yet reduced many a talented craftsman to a state of jittering self-consciousness.

Literature was almost entirely in the hands of the Romantic school. Coleridge, Southey and Wordsworth were established poets. Byron was a hero. Sentimental keepsake annuals flooded the bookshops. Thomas Moore and Alaric A. Watts were drawing-room idols. Sir Walter Scott gave an impetus to reviving Gothic architecture which was far greater than that given by the whimsicalities of Walpole and Beckford. The popular style for the newest fashionable architecture was Perpendicular. In painting, this taste is expressed in the works of Cattermole and Joseph Nash and Prout. Scholars were taking to British antiquarianism.

1867

Just when it looked as though Boggleton was going to become one of those decayed market towns which would have been no credit to an age of progress and prosperity like the mid-nineteenth century, fortune saved it from oblivion. The Great Junction Railway decided that a site near Boggleton was a suitable place for its works. So in 1850 a town was built called New Boggleton. This consisted at first of several rows of workmen's dwellings with a central green space, a church, an institute and some shops.

Enterprising Boggletonians from the old town erected an arcade of shops at the edge of the new town. A farmer sold off his land to a speculator who proceeded to erect as many houses on it as he could fit in. Then there were no town-planning laws to stop him. New Boggleton spread until it met Old Boggleton, and the small houses at the London end of the High Street came down under the onward rush of the new town.

The new works were a magnificent sight: a glimpse into the engine rooms showed vista upon vista of machines with men toiling happily at them. The GJR built a huge viaduct across the valley outside the town. The old naval captain in one of the genteel houses by the abbey – he was the last survivor of the original inhabitants of the group – thought that the viaduct was magnificent, comparable to the abbey itself, symbolizing the strength and beauty of engineering in cast iron and brick against the architecture of the Middle Ages. But he was a sensible man always in touch with the times.

The new rector (high church: instituted a weekly Communion instead of the old quarterly administration of the Sacrament) was deeply opposed to the building of the viaduct. He tried to agitate with the mayor and corporation. But they were all for humouring the railway since big profits were to be made out of it. Only a few landowners sympathized with the rector and agreed that the viaduct ruined the venerable and picturesque appearance of the abbey. So the rector had to content himself with medievalizing his parish church. The old box pews were taken down and nice sticky pitch-pine ones of a Christian shape substituted. The windows were filled with coloured glass from Hardman's works. The screen across the chancel and north chapel was removed because it blocked the view of the new chancel. The high pulpit was destroyed and a new one made out of the remains of the screen. The hatchments were removed and the plaster stripped from the walls.

The Nonconformists were no less active. But since the established church liked Gothic, they preferred the Italian style. The new independent chapel, now called Congregational, was of white brick with red brick dressings and in an ornate but inexpensive Romanesque manner.

The Adamsbec family had long ago sold Boggleton House to a prosperous shop-owner who gutted the interior and built warehouses in the garden. Plate glass took the place of the old square-paned windows and only a few of the more old-fashioned tradesmen who were unable to keep up with the new influx and increased competition regretted the passing of Old Boggleton.

The railway brought with it newer manufactories, and more chapels and churches sprung up. On the hills outside the town a smartish suburb was built for the foremen and higher clerical people connected with the factories. The richest people of all built themselves huge country houses near the town: houses in the Jacobean style and the Italian style with high walls and iron gates with lamp-posts on either side of the drive and a crest on the top of each. One of the most prosperous of these rich men founded the Boggleton Art Gallery, which has some of the largest pictures in England on its walls depicting Crimean scenes, Highland cattle, historical occasions and various other subjects calculated to turn the minds of Boggleton mechanics from the contemplation of the machinery and urban scenery by which they were surrounded.

Old Boggleton and New Boggleton became a large town of 100,000 inhabitants and the only remains of Old Boggleton were the town hall and the Quaker meeting house, while some cottages near the church still survived in a derelict condition as a memorial to the oldest Boggleton of all.

The machine gets into its stride

The tradition of craftsmanship was supplanted by the machine. The Great Exhibition of 1851 had shown that many objects could be made by machine at a quarter the cost and just as well as those made by hand. The set rules of colour and design pervading in 1836 had not been forgotten and the exhibits of 1851 in the late-lamented Crystal Palace were still worthy of the study of the fastidious. It is fashionable now to laugh at the Great Exhibition. It is a pity that this humour does not extend to the exhibits displayed today in the windows of the multiple stores.

While the machine was still a symbol of progress (whatever progress might be) to the majority, it was terrifying to many intellectuals. The Oxford Movement in the Church had given Gothic architecture official approval. Gothic was medieval. The Middle Ages were the days of crafts-men and Christianity. Therefore the machine was un-Christian. Classical architecture was pagan. Individuality was sacred. Pugin and, later, Ruskin supported this reaction from the machine. The pre-Raphaelites, now established, were the men of the moment. Art had caught up with literature. Even railway stations were built in the medieval style. The Grand Tour was supplanted by a visit to Belgium and the Gothic cathedrals of France. Venetian Gothic was imitated even in the main streets of London.

1907

About this time the Radicals in the town decided to improve the lot of the workers in the packed streets down by the railway works and other factories. An Evening Institute was founded, built in the new art style of Gothic (by the architect of the new Wesleyan church). Lectures were given on the ruined abbey (which was carefully patched up and the grass round it mowed and planted with beds of geraniums, a small admission fee being charged), on Italian painting, socialism, eugenics, eurythmics, hygiene, economics and other important subjects. The old cottages near the church were rebuilt in an even more ancient style than they had been in before.

The Conservatives decided to improve the civic dignity of Boggleton. The plain town hall was pulled down and a handsome edifice in Portland stone and in the Viennese Baroque manner arose in its place, surmounted by a tower with illuminated clock faces.

Ivy was planted along the buttresses of the railway viaduct to make it harmonize with the abbey. The false stucco villas by the abbey were at last taken down: a terrace of houses was put up by a speculator on a site nearer the abbey itself, so that they would have commanded no view, anyway. The tram service was extended to the abbey gates.

The rector's wife was an artistic woman and taught blob work (watercolours) in the Institute and sent her daughters to Bedales. The municipal art gallery made her and her daughters laugh. They presented the Melville, the Sims and the Whistler to the gallery.

Boggleton had changed the colour of its buildings, just as it had changed the colour of its politics, to pink. Only the Quaker meeting house remained the same.

The Morris movement

The Classical tradition never died. Greek in 1837, Italianate in 1867, 'Queen Anne' (Norman Shaw) in 1897, neo-Renaissance (Blomfield, Sir Ernest George, Belcher, Alfred Drury and various other sculptors of public monuments) in 1907.

The Gothic revival transmogrified itself. There could be too much medievalism. William Morris realized that the movement needed a political as well as a religious background. Guild socialism was the result. But Morris's insistence on hand processes, though often admirable for those rich enough to afford the price, led to various repulsive imitations. Sham beams, sham lanterns, sham Morris wallpapers spread rapidly. The productions of the Kelmscott Press, never legible, did little good to the few lingering traditions of English printing and typography. To counterbalance these bad effects, the Morris movement really did stimulate reaction to and criticism of many machine-made products, particularly furniture. The movement simplified designs and insisted on the simple life. From it sprang the Garden Cities, the C. F. A. Voysey, early Lutyens and Baillie Scott small houses, and later the Art Nouveau movement. Daring radicalism, fresh air, the works of H. G. Wells, unstained oak, white nurseries, child welfare work. There was no hint of the Oxford Movement about the new Gothic revival. Much more a hint of free thought.

The Art Nouveau people are responsible for contemporary architecture at its best. George Walton and C. R. Mackintosh, who came from the famous Glasgow School, built in a style which was soon taken up in Germany. Only in its decorative features, such as ironwork and stencilling, did their architecture seem any different from the truly modern architecture of today. It is ironic that the simplicity of the Crystal Palace should have been reached out of a movement indirectly inspired by that Gothic revival which was, in its inception, inimical to the machine age which the Palace glorified.

Painting in England, with the death of the pre-Raphaelites, dwindled into unimportance. France took the lead. Here and there the old tradition of good English water-colours hung on. But most of the work was either decorative Art Nouveau (Aubrey Beardsley in the 'nineties and Frank Brangwyn, who is a lesser Baillie Scott) or in a style which is still identified with the portraits in the Royal Academy. Whistler was the last giant, and he was an American.

1937

Boggleton's period of prosperity was nearly over when orders for armaments brought temporary relief to some of the factories. The Adamsbecs have sold their country house as a building estate: their pictures fetched very little. The trams have been replaced by buses. Two of the Nonconformist chapels have been sold to chain stores. The Bedalian daughters of the late rector have opened an 'olde' tea place in one of the cottages near the church. The big merchants' houses outside the town have become a lunatic asylum, a hospital and municipal offices. Their grounds have been turned into a public park.

The population is being moved out of the crowded streets near the station. Some are being moved into council houses put up on a nice but rather waterlogged site near the abbey. Others who can afford it are going into some of the lovely new villas which are being erected all round the town. Each one is different, the beams being very cleverly arranged. Stained-glass windows may be found in all of them, parlour or non-parlour type. True the walls are thin, the wood of the doors is unseasoned, the foundations are bad, the chimneys smoke, there is not enough accommodation, but on the other hand every garden has a low wall and crazy paving, and the interior fittings are in an up-to-date jazz modern style.

There are hardly any prosperous local tradesmen as the big shops are all run by London combines. Motors have brought prosperity to the Georgian Dolphin Hotel, which has rebuilt itself in the Tudor style in order to keep up with the times. The Institute is not doing so well now that culture comes via the wireless and cinema.

I am afraid we have not much time for art in Boggleton, though art criticism is quite popular with some of us. A Frank Brangwyn of a steel works was bought out of trust money by the committee of the municipal art gallery, but it was thought a little old-fashioned. Several young artists have been painting the viaduct for their commercial art course. The Boggleton Surrealist has found the large canvases in the art gallery interesting. Art, like the rest of the town, is controlled from London; there is no distinctive native talent, just as there is now no native craftsmanship.

Boggleton itself takes up much more room than it should do. In 1837 you could see the meadows and elms between the houses in the High Street: now you will have to go at least a mile in any direction to see a tree at all – and even then the fields will have a municipal appearance and the burnt grass will be bright with pieces of paper.

The Jazz Age and modern opportunities

Never has there been such a time for opportunities as now, and never have they been so missed. Architecture is dominated by the neo-Renaissance of 1906, and illustrious architects like Sir Herbert Baker, whose Bank of England and South Africa House speak for themselves. Another big school is the even less satisfactory pseudo-modern as typified by the new University Library at Cambridge, the jazz Egyptian of factories by Wallis Gilbert & Partners, and the pseudo-Swedish of the work of Edward Maufe and Grey Wornum, the architects for middlebrows.

Furniture is mostly still pseudo-Jacobean or, worse still, pseudo-modern, without even any Swedish about it. Textiles show a certain amount of improvement, more often in their texture than their design. But 'jazz' 1925 meaningless juxtaposition of arcs and angles is all too prevalent.

Painting is more hopeful. Artists are beginning to see the importance of representationalism, thanks to the Surrealists, and abstract art has given a sense of form and texture to our sight, which is sadly lacking in architecture. It would be impossible to chronicle the hundreds of schools of art and of art critics now existing in this country. A new style appears about once a month so that even art critics are bewildered by the harm they have assisted in doing.

The mass of styles and the lack of coherence are due to the bewilderment of man's mind. In 1836, religion was a force; the machine was another; both gave hope. In 1906, the machine was unpopular, and agnosticism and atheism had a religious sincerity about them. People had hope and they thought they knew what was wrong.

Today, the machine has given us everything we want – steel, glass and concrete for houses, hundreds of stuffs for textiles, varieties of pigmentation, processing of wood, processing of stone. But no one knows what to believe. Fear dominates the political world and affects artists, always the most sensitive if not the most practical of people. Greed keeps the artist out and even keeps common sense out. The speculative builder ruins the landscape and builds potential slums. The commercial master showers junk on us from multiple stores and governs his assistants by fear. Time is misunderstood. There is an idea that we must save it! Save it for what?

That our buildings and paintings and manufactured things may be the product of half-digested theories of art – as half-digested as the luncheons we eat, with our eyes on the clock. The machine is discredited, God is discredited, human nature is discredited. We are turning ourselves into the material of which slaves are made – time slaves, machine slaves and money slaves.

There is one hope only for the improvement in design and that is, odd as it may seem, a spiritual change in the people. The company inflators must be deflated, time must be slowed down, anxiety must be removed so that we can think and see things in perspective. Then it will be possible to undo the harm, to plan what has been unplanned, to use the materials which the machine has given us to their best advantage.

We have certain glimpses of what can be done. There was the Crystal Palace; there are the designs of our motor cars when they are not full of bogus streamlining, the faint tremor of the public conscience about slums and the distressed areas, the attempt to save what is left of England from the speculator and the commercial gentleman, a few blocks of flats in highbrow suburbs, the poetry of Yeats and Eliot, the improvement in poster design – these are about all.

Church-crawling

Leader Magazine, 23 April 1949

My old motor car naturally slows down as it passes a church. Trained by long association with this middle-aged church-crawler, it stops at the gate and gives him time to scan the notice board and see whether the church is one of the low kind which is locked. And one of the first things the beginner needs to know is where to find the key if the church *is* locked. It may be behind the notice board in the porch, on the wall plate, among the spiders in the roof of the porch, in the lamp-holder or under the mat. Failing that, it is probably in the nearest house to the church. Increase of crime has led many incumbents to lock churches. Personally I think this shows a lack of Faith, Hope and Charity and that there are better arguments for keeping churches open than there are for locking them.

No one has ever counted how many Anglican places of worship there are in England. The number is thought to be about 20,000. The most I have ever seen in one long summer day is 16. I should think I see on an average 3 a week which I have not seen before. At that rate it will take me about 128 years to see all there are in England, even supposing I have the money, petrol and leisure to complete the task.

There are three ways of looking at a church – as a place of worship, as a historical record, as architecture. No church of the thousands I have visited has been wholly 'devoid of interest' as the guide books say. This is because always they can be considered as places of worship. Christians believe that the only date in history which is not a mere figure is the birth of Christ. At that time the Creator of the Universe became a man and dwelt in time. On that date Eternity came into time. Many of us believe that the Creator continues to dwell in time in the Church he founded. On this belief the old churches of England were built. While the human race flows like a tide into Eternity, leaving dead bodies behind it, Eternity waits in churches, however hideous they may be. For this reason the date of a church has never seemed to me all-important. In the eyes of Eternity, what are the thousand years between say, the Saxon church of Brixworth, Northampton (AD 670), and St Philip's, Cosham (AD 1937)?

This is not the place to describe the nature of worship in the Church of England, enjoyable though that would be, so I move at once to churches as history.

There is no such thing as an average English church. Each differs vastly from that in the next parish. I will, however, try to invent a church which must stand for all old churches, and some characteristics of it may be seen in the nearest old church to you – by 'old' I mean going back to Norman times, which many thousands do. I will call it Bagby St Petroc, a Lincolnshire and Danish sounding place name with a Cornish saint's name added to it – a bit of east and west at once. The historical way of looking at a church is all a hunt for significant detail. It is detective work. As we go up the churchyard path to enter, as is usual in most parts of England, by a south door, we see all the older headstones on this, the south side of the graveyard. They are of local stone like the church and have beautifully inscribed lettering, all curls and tails, cherubs, skulls and hour-glasses carved in relief; and the earliest we can see are unlikely to be older than 1700. Medieval poor were buried without headstones and not very deep. Their names were remembered in prayers at mass rather than in lettered stone, however finely cut. On the other, the north, side of the church stand Victorian tombs of white marble, and the most depraved designs of all will be the modern ones. The monumental mason of the eighteenth century was an artist and craftsman. I hope he will one day become one again.

St Petroc's Church looks almost new outside. This is because the Victorians took the pebbledash off the walls, repointed the stone beneath with grey cement, stuck blue slates on the roof and gave them red ridge tiles and generally tidied the building. The present century leaves its mark with wires clamped clumsily onto a beautiful old west tower, the noblest feature of the outside of the church, so that the building looks as though it is on the telephone, though it is really only on the electric grid whose light ruins most old churches with its hard, metallic stare.

The stone tracery of the windows too, is mostly hard and sharp, meaning the Victorians renewed it, though two windows survive perhaps with stone tracery softened by time. To distinguish old stone from new is easy. One has only to use one's eyes. Old stone is weathered by time and sometimes has mason's marks cut on it or scratch dials – a circle like a clock face, the lower half only cut into grooves with a hole in the centre for the gnomon. Those with holes along the circumference were probably a means whereby the priest showed what time the next mass was going to be. He put a stick into the appropriate hole.

Bagby St Petroc has a trusting rector, so the church is open. As we enter we notice that the south entrance door under the porch is Norman with a round head to it and zigzags carved on the outer of the three rows of little stones which form the door's arch. We step down into the church, so the graveyard probably has risen with its centuries of layers of dead.

Now, while you sit in a shiny deal pew and survey the grey walls which have been stripped of their plaster and pointed like the outside so that the church looks as though it has been skinned, I am going to sink us back into former centuries. Sit in the middle of the church, that is to say, the nave, and face east towards the high altar. All old English churches face east.

Almost everything you can see at present is Victorian, the stained glass (much of it finely designed and boldly coloured), the stone tracery (much of it a faithful reconstruction of what was there before), the chancel and altar fittings, the shining tiled floor, the choir stalls, the organ blocking up the northeast corner of the church, the vestry blocking up the southeast corner, the pews you sit in – all except these grand clustered columns to left and right of you, stretching away to the east end and, perhaps, a nobly sculptured monument up in the chancel where a lady gracefully carved in white marble weeps over a simple stone urn.

This last will be eighteenth-century when all the greatest sculptors carved church monuments and signed them usually on the left or right hand bottom corner. There may be some older pieces of stone-work, the font, or a niche here and there. But nearly everything is Victorian.

Sit in the same place and see Bagby church on a Sunday morning 11 a.m., 150 years ago. The building grows much lighter; clear leaded panes, oblong shaped, are in all the windows. Your pew rises with you so that you can only just see over the top of it. It has a door and it is much larger and lined inside with green baize and it has seats round three sides. Above the chancel arch hang the royal arms, painted as well as the best inn sign. The walls are of white plaster. Even the noble columns, which alone you recognize, are whitewashed. A white ceiling is above you instead of that open pitchpine roof. You are warm and comfortable. But you cannot kneel. You can only lean forward and pray into your beaver hat. An orchestra tunes up behind you and as you glance round you see a west gallery behind and above you with the village choir with fiddles, bassoon and a conductor with a tuning fork.

The squire and his lady arrive by a special entrance into a huge box pew with a fireplace in that corner where the vestry was, and above them are the marble monuments of the squire's father and grandfather. The rector climbs up into a huge three-decker in front of you. He goes only half way up. Below him sits the clerk who says a loud Amen at the end of each prayer. The rector will ascend yet higher to the pulpit itself only to preach. He wears a black gown with white bands at his throat.

The church is full. Bonnets and heads appear above pews and people are facing from all directions, towards the pulpit. The chancel is empty, though you can see it through a screen which crosses that chancel arch. The screen is wooden and seems once to have been brightly painted. The altar, under the great commandment board below the east window, is covered with red velvet, and on it are two beautiful silver candlesticks. The candles are not lit, for this is not a sacrament Sunday. The rector glances around from his height. The sounding board over the pulpit above him looks as though it will fall down on his head. He glances towards the galleries where the choir is and where the charity children sit in their quaint uniforms. 'Dearly beloved brethren . . .' – we are away, through the familiar prayer book service of Morning Prayer.

Bagby St Petroc Church fades back another three centuries, and we see it as it has been newly rebuilt in 1480 in shape, and with windows, very much as we saw it when we first stepped in under that Norman arch. It is eleven in the morning, but all masses will be over for the usual time was nine o'clock. Perhaps there has been a saint's holy day, for these were always occurring in England, three or four a month besides Sundays. There will be no pew for you to sit in, perhaps a bench with curved ends. But I think we can safely assume that the only seats are stone benches along the aisle walls, to which the weakest may go. So you will have to kneel on the stone floor, for there, hanging over the high altar and glimpsed with a light burning before it, through the tracery of the gilded and brightly coloured screen, hangs the pyx.

This silver vessel, veiled with rich lace, contains the consecrated Host, the spiritual presence of our Lord Himself, and you will be thought a blasphemer and unnatural if you are not on your knees before it. The church will be smelling of crushed yew and aromatic herbs which were strewn over the floor for the feast. Immense, hanging over the centre of that painted screen, will be a wooden figure of Our Lord on the Cross, Our Lady and St John standing either side of Him. This is the rood.

Wherever you look, sacred pictures and emblems will meet your eye. A figure of St Petroc in a niche, the plastered walls covered with paintings, St Christopher to your left over the north door, Bible scenes all over the south wall, heaven and hell on the woodwork behind the rood; all the windows will be filled with painted glass of the time, with much silver stain in it which glows gold and many little figures of blue and red and green on a whitish background.

As you look up to the oak roof, you will see angels carved where the rafters spring, and the roof above will be studded with coloured bosses, some of them comic, some sacred, some coarse and all coloured. Everywhere there are people, for here, this side of the screen is the people's part of the church. The noise of men arguing is going on in the porch, a usual place for business; one of the priests is teaching a school in the little room over the porch. And all around you are men and women on their knees praying. Praying in these days is as natural as breathing. No one thinks it odd. Some infants, too young for school, are playing hide and seek among the columns to left and right of you. Some women behind you are gossiping in loud voices.

The truth is, the nave of the church is social hall, theatre, library, meeting place of the whole village. Except for the few rich, all lived in such squalor that none of their cottages have survived. The old cottages we still see in some villages are never earlier than seventeenth century. Before that they were little more than mud huts with thatched roofs, used for begetting, eating, sleeping and dying. The church was home.

Now walk up to the screen painted with saints on its panels and look through. The high altar is hung with curtains and its frontal with jewelled cloth. Behind it is a carved piece of alabaster, stretching its whole length, gilded and depicting scenes of the Passion. There are no candles or ornaments on the altar except at service time. Through screens on either side of it you will see other equally rich altars each with a lamp burning in front of it. In the southeast corner is the chantry altar and chapel of the landlord of the village, ancestor of the squire you saw 300 years later. This medieval landlord employs a priest to say mass daily for the souls of his ancestors. That chanting priest is just now putting away coloured vestments in a huge oak chest.

In the north chapel, divided off from the chancel, as the south chapel is, by a painted screen called a parclose, is another chapel. It belongs to the trade guild of woolcombers, for Bagby is in a wool district, and is dedicated to their patron saint. They also pay for a priest, for the trade is flourishing. And in other parts of the church there may be altars belonging to other guilds, trade and religious. Since it is a holy day, you may hear the thump of a ball against the buttresses of the tower, as the young men play fives against it.

It is as well you have moved as far up the church as the screen, for I am going to sink us back another three centuries. Bagby St Petroc Church in 1180 is small indeed. No aisles, no tower, no side chapels, no guilds, no pillared nave, no pointed arches, and half its length. You are in a Norman building. The nave is high and dark and thick-walled. In the feeble light which comes through on to the stone floor from little round-headed windows sunk deep and high up in the walls and keeping out the weather with slats of wood or transparent horn, you may just descry red and blue paintings everywhere. They are in the style of the mosaics we see on Italian churches. There is no screen now. That round Norman arch is the chief eastern feature of the nave. It is the entrance to the dark and mysterious chancel which has a semicircular east wall or apse.

Here there is a small round-headed stained window. The glass is thick and dark and stiff, with heavy black lines. It is more like a small transparent mosaic than those light wide windows of three centuries later. The chancel is tiled. The altar stands away from the east wall, and there is possibly a low stone reredos behind it. The altar is supported on four stone pillars and draped with a cloth. One has the feeling that this is a mission church to natives and that the old heathen superstitions are fighting to get in.

Go back another three centuries and you may find a church here still, built by the Saxons and of wood – for except for one little wooden church in Essex, only their *stone* buildings survive. Then the same faith was taught and life was freer, for the Danes and later the Normans had not conquered the country. And if it was a Celtic rather than a Saxon church, as it probably would have been if Bagby St Petroc were in the west or north of England, the church may well have been rich and beautiful within, though very small. And before that, perhaps, the site was a pagan burial ground.

The third way of looking at a church, as architecture, affords me, at any rate, great pleasure. But it is a pleasure derived from practice. Once I thought everything old was beautiful. This is not true. Then in reaction I looked only at Georgian buildings – and there are many fine Georgian churches in the towns and in the country. Then I went back to the Romanesque style in which Saxons and Normans built. Many of their buildings survive – but only a few of them are complete. About a half dozen Saxon and a few Norman churches, though there are thousands with Norman remains in them.

Gothic architecture was born in the great abbey churches, not in parish churches, and it is in cathedrals and abbeys that one may see it at its best. As everyone knows, the Gothic style originated from the need to vault a wide oblong in stone. And stone was preferred for roofs, because it lessened the risk of fire. Not that the Romanesque builders of Norman and earlier times were unaware of how to do stone vaulting, but they were tradition-ally imitating the architecture of the Roman Empire, whose only arch was a round arch. They could make semicircular vaults and quadripartite vaults, that is to say two semicircular vaults of equal height intersecting at right angles. To vault a large oblong in stone was beyond their power. In this country the earliest surviving attempt to solve the problem is thought to be at the Benedictine Abbey of Durham (now Durham Cathedral) *c.* 1100. But such experiments could only be made in the large abbeys which flourished in England after the Norman Conquest until the coming of the friars.

Many of these abbeys have now become cathedrals, though they were never intended for vast congregations but rather for processions and many masses said, often simultaneously, at different altars. When one reads in a description of a village church that there is an E.E. piscina or a Dec. arcade, one may look with reverence at its antiquity, and pleasure at any mouldings and carving. But the structural problems which gave rise to these early styles and which gave them their full meaning and grace are not usually found in village churches.

The only approach to the noble medieval buildings is to be found in some of the great Victorian churches of our towns and suburbs. They do not depend on age or atmosphere or historical interest or texture for their beauty, but simply on 'firmnesse, commodity and delight', that is to say on architecture. As clever constructions, ingenious and original plans, as well-proportioned designs, arch relating to roof and window, moulding to arch, and decorative detail to general effect, they are unsur-passed. A Victorian church wholly by G. E. Street, J. L. Pearson, G. F. Bod-ley, H. Woodyer, W. White, J. D. Sedding, W. Butterfield, Bidlake, Austin and Paley or Temple Moore, is always worth sitting in, looking at and absorbing. They took up Gothic where the Middle Ages left it and developed styles of their own. Their last living survivor, J. N. Comper, is also their successor. He built what is to me the finest new parish church in England – St Mary's, Wellingborough, Northants.

The instruments you need for church-crawling are (1) a notebook in which you can sketch and write remarks; (2) opera or field glasses for viewing roofs and stained glass; (3) a one-inch map; (4) most important, an unprejudiced eye.

Christian architecture

Britain Today, February 1951

There was recently a great fuss in *The Times* and in the frustrated pro-
fession of architecture about the new building of Coventry Cathedral.
Much publicity was given to the Chapel of Unity which the new Cathedral
is to contain and which will serve members of the Anglican and free
churches (the free churches being the Nonconformists).

> Let's build a great cathedral
> For England's rising youth,
> A free and easy temple
> Of undogmatic truth,

says the Reverend S. J. Forrest, an Anglican lampoonist, and he might well
be referring to the all-embracing 'goodwill' behind the promoters of
Coventry Cathedral. In the final verse of his highly amusing poem he
says:

> There's room for brave agnostic
> For Hindu or Parsee,
> Or devotee of Islam
> (So *very* C. of E.),
> And if uniting parties
> At Bishops take offence
> We'll consecrate the ladies
> And take our orders thence!

Among the public there is a vague feeling that there ought to be a cathedral
and that it ought to be religious but it does not matter really what kind
of religion so long as there is general goodwill all round. But those who
really care about knowing their Creator and obeying His demands are
bothered by the new building. Is it to be a preaching house or is it to be
a house where God abides in the Blessed Sacrament? Architects, writing
merely professionally, have evaded the issue by concentrating on a battle
of the styles which is no longer Gothic versus Classic but Gothic versus
something vaguely called the modern style.

Now the truth is that there is no modern style in England. There is a flashy international decorative treatment which ruins the main streets of our towns. It comes from America, Berlin, Paris and Leicester and expresses itself in plate-glass shop fronts and repulsive imitation marbles made of various synthetic substances. It is called 'modern'. There is also a more serious kind of building in this country which fulfils a need instead of trying to create one, and that is to be found in housing. It is temporary housing and it expresses the temporary nature of our present stage of industrialism. To describe prefabs, of whatever type or material, as being in any particular style would be rather like bothering about the style of a cowshed. They were put up because they had to be put up and that was all.

A great architectural style is only produced when a people is settled and convinced. It is at its best when every craftsman is an artist. Today, we of the mechanical world find aesthetic pleasure in the hand-made tools and toys and domestic utensils of agricultural tribes in Africa and the East which some old-fashioned people still call 'primitive'. But that pleasure is primarily an expression of our own longing to use our hands in producing beautiful things as our forbears did in almost every department of life until about the year 1840. Nor was there any sudden cessation. The tradition of craftsmanship went on in England unconsciously in many trades, but unfortunately the inspiration which the Church gave to art died when Europe ceased to be Christendom and became a continent of growing jealous nations.

The building of churches in Britain today is given a subsidiary place. Houses come first, churches afterwards. In Christendom it was the other way round. 'The pious English' of Christendom are commemorated all over our island by thousands of medieval churches. Almost every village has its old church, probably Norman in origin, first a dependant on the nearest abbey and later a separate cure of souls. And as the wool trade flourished in the later middle ages, this church probably grew to large dimensions, especially if it were in East Anglia or the vast limestone districts of England where building material was plentiful.

As the kings brought gold and frankincense and myrrh to the house of Our Lord, so did the pious English bring their costliest gifts to the churches. The buildings glowed with coloured glass and painted wooden screens and plaster walls and jewelled frontals. The church had to be the best building and it had to be better than the church of the neighbouring village. So village vied with village on who could build the highest church tower, who could have the largest stained-glass window. Naturally, in these conditions, a style developed. Gothic (and whether its origin was in France or England does not much matter for France and England were not consciously separate nations when the Gothic style started) – Gothic was the product of structural necessity. Fire, that great destroyer of old buildings, was continually eating the large wooden roofs of the Norman churches. Stone vaulting was preferable. It became necessary to vault an oblong space with stone. This could only be done by raising one pair of round arches supporting the oblong space higher than the pair at right angles to it. Hence the pointed arch, hence those beginnings of Gothic which may be seen in the great abbey churches of Durham and Fountains. Gothic was indeed engineering in stone. By the time the long first wave of church building had ceased in England, that is to say in about 1500, stone was being used almost as iron was used centuries later in the great railway stations of the Victorian age.

The English Perpendicular style was designed to show stained glass and internal wood carving to the greatest advantage. Therefore, walls had to be little more than glass screens. The greatest English building of the late medieval times, in fact almost early Renaissance, is King's College Chapel, Cambridge, and this, in terms of engineering, is a vast marquee whose screen walls containing their hundreds of square feet of coloured glass are no more structurally important than the canvas walls of a tent.

A delight in stone construction continued in England throughout the seventeenth and eighteenth centuries, but it was turned more to the building of bridges and houses than of churches. What churches *were* built, such as those by the masters Wren, Hawksmoor and Gibbs, may have had Renaissance mouldings and details and shapes of the windows, but generally somewhere they have either a steeple or internal liturgical arrangement which remembers the Gothic age.

Then came the second great period of church building, in Victoria's time, when there was much dull copying of medieval work. Some of the most prominent architects, however, notably Street and Butterfield, realized that copying old Gothic was not really being Gothic at all. They were men of the Anglican Catholic tradition with a firm faith, reminding one of the pious English of the past. William Butterfield, the most daring experimenter of them all, realized in nineteenth-century London that he was living in a brick age and that if he was to build in the Gothic spirit he must build in brick. And Gothic does not lend itself to London brick so he built pointed churches out of bricks, but in order to compensate for the lack of external adornment that stone carving and internal painting had given to medieval buildings, he made his walls of coloured bricks arranged in patterns. These patterns emphasized the lines of construction.

There are today a few of the older church architects who represent the living church tradition. The greatest of these is Sir Ninian Comper, who always builds his churches from the altar outwards. He, like most members of the Church of England, is one who stresses the value of the Sacraments. So his churches are an expression of his own faith. Sometimes they are Gothic in style and sometimes Classic, but primarily they are designed to bring you to your knees when you see the altar through the mystery of screens or under the golden canopy of a vast ciborium.

To return to Coventry Cathedral – its purposes are all too vaguely expressed in the terms of the competition. A masterpiece will only come from a man of sincere belief. I am certain that 'style' is of no importance, beside reverence and humility. I know that we are no longer a nation of artists, as we were in the days when every detail could safely be left to the craftsmen concerned. Only the single genius of a man who can design and inspire in all departments of church art will produce a building which will shake the populace around it out of its indifference. In order to build such a building, he will have to be a man who believes that his gifts are from God and who offers them back in cathedral form in humility.

Design for a new cathedral

Daily Telegraph, 3 September 1951

Some people still think of a cathedral as the local church, only more so. The altar is further away, the stained glass windows are bigger, the services are longer and the choir is a bit bigger. Otherwise it is the same as ordinary 'church' with rather more people there and the sermon booming away through amplifiers hung like home-made wireless sets on the mighty columns of the nave.

Nothing could be further from the medieval purpose of a cathedral. It was never intended for a gigantic preaching place. Indeed, the public were not encouraged, except as lucrative pilgrims to shrines. The monks said masses at many altars in the early morning. The services went on in different parts of the building at the same time. Monks gathered for their daily offices in the choir, as the dean and canons still do in the choirs of our old cathedrals. Our great buildings were for the most part monastic.

In considering Mr Spence's design for the new Coventry Cathedral we must remember, before any preoccupation with style, the purpose of a cathedral, and St Michael's, Coventry, was never built as such. It was a town church raised to the status of cathedral in the present century. In the Middle Ages it had been a people's church, built and added to by the citizens of Coventry themselves. The girdlers, dyers, drapers, cappers and mercers had each built themselves chapels on to the church. They maintained the lights, gave the vestments, jewels and stained glass, ironwork and woodwork and paid their own priests. The butchers and marlers and other religious guilds built chapels onto Holy Trinity Church next door. The devotion of these tough and unemotional merchants and craftsmen is one of the shining jewels of medieval religion. They may have mingled superstition with their prayers to patron saints, but they gave of their best to their churches.

Mr Spence and the people who defined the rules of the competition were going back to the old tradition in wanting a building which was to represent Coventry. It would be no bad thing if the Christians employed by the motor, the bicycle and other great industries of Coventry each maintained a chapel in the new cathedral.

But such is not to be. The new design does not allow for more than three altars besides the main one. Great stress was laid on the provision of a Chapel of Unity where Nonconformists (excluding Roman Catholics) and our own Church might meet. Mr Spence has solved this problem very cleverly.

The ruined cathedral, like English churches almost without exception, had its altar at the east end. The new building is at right angles to the older cathedral and with its altar facing north. The ruins are to be retained and turned into a 'Garden of Rest', that is to say one of those places with municipal lawns where you are not quite sure whether it is sacrilegious to eat a picnic lunch among the rather over-preserved remains.

From the ruins it will be possible to glimpse through a series of glass screens the altar of the cathedral, which is below a blank wall hung with what will be the largest piece of tapestry in the world and not yet designed. The side walls of the new cathedral are a zigzag formation with windows shining towards the altar and therefore, when you are inside the building, and looking towards the altar, invisible. These zigzags are to contain something never heard of before called 'hallowing places'. Above them will be symbolical sculpture. One is roughly outlined in Mr Spence's designs. It shows 'Agriculture': a man in trousers digging a furrow, a symbolic tree, a medieval man below it and an angel in the sky.

Are worshippers meant to drop down on their knees in the 'hallowing place' – a shelf is provided and there is room for a chair or two – and say a prayer to Agriculture: 'O blessed Agriculture . . . ?' Or, in some other zigzag, to start, 'I beseech thee, holy Civics . . . ?' Surely such worship and such symbolism are a little remote and cold even for today? The walls of this great hall are to be of the lovely pinkish-grey local stone, both without and within. The thin pillars which support the shallow concrete vault are to be steel encased with concrete.

The best feature of this new cathedral seems to me to be the west-east axis, that is to say the view across the building. This is all to do with the 'Chapel of Unity'. Mr Spence has designed it as a star shape against his west wall, out of sight of the high altar but looking straight across to the font and main entrance. This is finely conceived.

But what is a 'Chapel of Unity'? It has no altar. Is it a place where we each agree to give up something which our Church holds sacred for the sake of getting on with another church? The result is surely a decreased creed for each of us just in order to be in the same room together on this earth. I am reminded of Gabriel Gillett's lines:

> See all from all men's point of view; use others' eyes to see with;
> And never preach what anyone could ever disagree with.

Mr Spence himself is an architect of imagination and with a sense of detail as well as plan, as his Sea and Ships Pavilion on the south bank and this cathedral fully testify. The good points of his design are the happy relation of the stern masses of his new building with the elegant thin ruins. The skyline is also carefully considered. His new buildings act as a contrasting solid to the soaring spire and pinnacles of the old church. His plan is ingenious and grows on one. His revival of the use of local stone is to be praised, and it is to be hoped that when he comes to use this stone he will dispense with the affectation of having no mouldings. For mouldings are as essential to throwing up the beauty and purpose of stonework as paint is to the body of a motor car.

But the building seems to me to be a failure because it is not a cathedral but a secular assembly hall with a font against one wall and an altar against another. The nave is too wide, the aisles are too narrow and too much depends on the artist who is chosen to design the huge tapestry above the high altar. The altar itself is too far away. It lacks mystery and the endlessness of vista upon vista characteristic of our faith itself. Compare it with Pearson's fine modern cathedral of Truro. It also lacks the rock-like look of Scott's Liverpool Cathedral. It is far below the original genius of Burges' Cathedral of St Finbar, Cork. It does not pray as a church should. Instead, it surprises like an exhibition building.

I do not think this is all the fault of Mr Spence but of the people who set the condition of the competition. They were so anxious that the building should be all things to all men that it expresses not a firm faith but a woolly goodwill. There is all the difference between being kind and believing something.

Our Church of England is a sacramental Church. We claim that it has apostolic succession. We stress the sacraments of baptism and holy communion. Many of us use the other sacraments which are available in our Church. We are a unity in ourselves. We have protestants and catholics among us. Our teaching is in our catechism and prayer book. Many millions have died in it. The cathedral should be a stronghold of our faith. But this building is too much an auditorium, too suggestive of an impracticable compromise, and we all know where compromise can lead us. Indeed, one of the 219 competitors, presumably aware of this, designed his cathedral wholly underground.

Altar, priest and people

Daily Telegraph, 28 July 1958

Three sorts of plan are being used today for new churches. The most usual is based on the Victorian innovation of putting a surpliced choir in the chancel. Thus the choir sits between the altar and the congregation. The congregation has a view of the altar and also of the profiles of the members of the choir. When the choir is extinct or absent, the congregation has a view of the sides of the choir stalls. The deeper the chancel, the farther the congregation is from the altar. At a celebration of the Holy Communion the parish priest is thus separated from his people.

The advantages of this arrangement are that the altar or table is in, as it were, a particularly sacred and set-apart portion of the church and a feeling of awe and mystery is created. Also, people are used to churches with chancels and there is much to be said for tradition. But for those coming to church for the first time, what goes on at the altar is remote, only partially visible and often inaudible.

The next most usual type is the 'dual-purpose' church on a new housing estate, used during the week for social functions, and with an altar behind a partition. The advantage of this sort of plan is that a parish priest, trying to build up a congregation, has somewhere to get to know his people and to bring them together on a less embarrassing level than that of religion. The disadvantage is that last night's cigarette smoke, litter and secular adornments such as dart boards and ping-pong tables have to be cleared away before the partition is drawn back for a service. Also, a purely secular hall can never have quite the same atmosphere as a church. There is something temporary about it.

In these days when most people have fairly decent houses to live in a church should be a church and a hall a hall. In medieval days, when the church was the only decent weatherproof building in the village and when cottages were little more than huts for sleeping in, the nave of the church was more naturally the social centre of the community.

The third sort of church has its altar in the middle of the congregation so that as many people as possible can see and hear what is going on there. In a new community where there are many who do not know about the sacraments of the Church and how they are administered, the parish priest needs to rivet attention by his actions.

Our greatest living church architect, Sir Ninian Comper, once said that a church should be planned from the altar outwards, and that the altar is the flame to which the church round it is a lantern. He himself re-designed a London church, St John's, Waterloo Road (since altered), and built St Philip's, Cosham, Portsmouth, each with its altar in the middle. His plan has been continued a step further by another experienced church architect, Mr T. Lawrence Dale, at St Swithun's, Kennington, a suburb of Oxford.

The altar stands in the middle of the new church under a canopy. The candlesticks on the altar are low so as not to obscure the actions of the parish priest from any side. The southern arm of the church is used as a chapel during the week, and the seats here can be turned round to face the high altar for big services.

The disadvantages of this plan are that some of the mystery and awe surrounding the Holy Communion is lost because the altar is so near the people. But the advantages, in the opinion of most parish priests to whom I have spoken on this subject, outweigh the disadvantages. The parish priest can teach the faith by holding attention with word, action and music all in harmony. When this kind of alertness is achieved all the mystery comes back – this time in the midst of the people, instead of far away from them.

Bell-ringing

from *Collins Guide to English Parish Churches* (1958)

Let us enter the church by the tower door and climb to the ringing chamber where the ropes hang through holes in the roof. Nowhere outside England except for a very few towers in the rest of the British Isles, America and the Dominions, are bells rung so well. The carillons of the Netherlands and of Bourneville and Atkinson's scent shop in London are not bell-ringing as understood in England. Carillon-ringing is done either by means of a cylinder worked on the barrel-organ and musical box principle, or by keyed notes played by a musician. Carillon bells are sounded by pulling the clapper to the rim of the bell. This is called chiming, and it is not ringing.

Bell-ringing in England is known among ringers as 'the exercise', rather as the rearing and training of pigeons is known among the pigeon fraternity as 'the fancy'. It is a classless folk art which has survived in the Church despite all arguments about doctrine and the diminution of congregations. In many a church when the parson opens with the words 'Dearly beloved brethren, the Scripture moveth us in sundry places...' one may hear the tramp of the ringers descending the newel stair into the refreshing silence of the graveyard. Though in some churches they may come in later by the main door and sit in the pew marked 'Ringers Only', in others they will not be seen again, the sweet melancholy notes of 'the exercise' floating out over the Sunday chimney-pots having been their contribution to the glory of God. So full of interest and technicality is the exercise that there is a weekly paper devoted to it called *The Ringing World*.

A belfry where ringers are keen has the used and admired look of a social club. There, above the little bit of looking-glass in which the ringers slick their hair and straighten their ties before stepping down into the outside world, you will find blackboards with gilded lettering proclaiming past peals rung for hours at a stretch. In another place will be the rules of the tower written in a clerkly hand. A charming Georgian ringers' rhyme survives at St Endellion, Cornwall, on a board headed with a picture of ringers in knee-breeches:

We ring the Quick to Church and dead to Grave
Good is our use, such usage let us have
Who here therefore doth Damn, or Curse or Swear,
Or strike in Quarrel thogh no Blood appear,
Who wears a Hall or Spurr or turns a Bell
Or by unskilful handling spoils a Peal,
Shall Sixpence pay for every single Crime
'Twill make him careful 'gainst another time.
Let all in Love and Friendship hither come,
Whilst the shrill Treble calls to Thundering Tom,
And since bells are our modest Recreation
Let's Rise and Ring and Fall to Admiration.

Many country towers have six bells. Not all these bells are medieval. Most were cast in the seventeenth, eighteenth or nineteenth centuries when change-ringing was becoming a country exercise. And the older bells will have been re-cast during that time, to bring them into tune with the new ones. They are likely to have been again re-cast in modern times and the ancient inscription preserved and welded on to the re-cast bell. Most counties have elaborately produced monographs about their church bells. The older bells have beautiful lettering sometimes, as at Somerby and South Somercotes in Lincolnshire, where they are inscribed with initial letters decorated with figures so that they look like illuminated initials from old manuscripts interpreted in relief on metal. The English love for Our Lady survived in inscriptions on church bells long after the Reformation, as did the use of Latin. Many eighteenth- and even early nineteenth-century bells have Latin inscriptions. A rich collection of varied dates may be seen by struggling about on the wooden cage in which the bells hang among the bat-droppings in the tower.

Many local customs survive in the use of bells. In some places a curfew is rung every evening; in others a bell is rung at five in the morning during Lent. Fanciful legends have grown up about why they are rung, but their origin can generally be traced to the divine offices. The passing bell is rung differently from district to district. Sometimes the years of the deceased are tolled, sometimes the ringing is three strokes in succession followed by a pause. There are instances of the survival of prayers for the departed where the bell is tolled as soon as the news of the death of a parishioner reaches the incumbent.

Who has heard a muffled peal and remained unmoved? Leather bags are tied to one side of the clapper and the bells ring alternately loud and soft, the soft being an echo, as though in the next world, of the music we hear on earth.

I make no apology for writing so much about church bells. They ring through our literature, as they do over our meadows and roofs and few remaining elms. Some may hate them for their melancholy, but they dislike them chiefly, I think, because they are reminders of Eternity. In an age of faith they were messengers of consolation.

The bells are rung down, the ting-tang will ring for five minutes, and now is the time to go into church.

Stained glass comes back

The Times, 25 May 1962

A delight of the new Coventry Cathedral is the element of surprise. Outside it rises a great pink sandstone fortress of beautiful masonry and dominates the city rather as the castle dominates Edinburgh. Inside it is all delicately modulated light, and never since King's College Chapel, Cambridge, was completed in the early sixteenth century has there been such a huge display of stained glass.

In Coventry the stained glass dominates, and it is interesting to compare this interior with that of another modern cathedral – Guildford – where stained glass is used so sparingly that one might almost think that it was a little wicked and should only be used discreetly.

There are two reasons for this change in attitude to stained glass. One is to do with modern methods of construction where buildings, instead of having thick brick or stone walls and little openings for light, are becoming more like tents whose curtain walls between the supporting poles to the lightly constructed roof become sheets of glass instead of canvas. There is an analogy here with English Perpendicular of the fifteenth century.

When Mr Robin Darwin reorganized the Royal College of Art in South Kensington he realized that stained glass needed to be something more than transparent pictures of angels and cherubs floating about in acres of clear glass, so dearly loved by diocesan advisory committees, and that the Good Shepherds and watery armorial designs turned out in their hundreds by commercial church furnishers were getting a bad name for what once was a great art. Two pupils, Geoffrey Clarke and Keith New, were making modern designs with deep rich colours. They were inspired no doubt by Léger and Matisse in France and at home by the work of Wilhelmina Geddes, of Belfast, and Evie Hone, of Dublin, who in turn were influenced by Harry Clark, the Tower of Glass Works, and Douglas Strachan who made much original and exciting glass in what might be called a nouveau-Celtic manner at the beginning of this century.

With Lawrence Lee, the head of the stained glass department at the Royal College, Messrs Clarke & New designed the nave windows for

Coventry. At this time too John Piper, who had from his youth made tracings of medieval stained glass, turned to the making of stained glass with Patrick Reyntiens as collaborator and executant. One result is their magnificent baptistry window at Coventry that has no representational figures at all, but makes its effect by subtly contrasting colours on a grand scale through the hundreds of oblongs provided by the architect. Another method of using stained glass, setting it in concrete instead of lead, which derives from the continent, is used at Coventry by Margaret Traherne in the Chapel of Unity.

This too short history of latest developments leads to a second reason for the change in modern stained glass – fashion in colour. Stained glass has never been a lost art, but the juxtaposition of its colours has changed with the centuries – and even by decades. In the thirties we were afraid of any colour at all except pastel shades, and this is shown in Guildford Cathedral. Modern artists in stained glass find more kinship with Chartres and Bourges and Canterbury and the early Victorian work of Cottingham, Hardman and Clutterbuck than they do with the glass at Fairford and King's Chapel.

Fashion will change but there is no doubt that the glass at Coventry will make people realize that stained glass is part of architecture and not an after-thought provided by church furnishers with hymn books and brass vases.

London's least-tasted pleasure

Illustrated London News, June 1971

Church-going is one of London's greatest and least-tasted pleasures. There are those who think church-going is a duty and that it is wicked to enjoy it. They must be warped puritan. The great advantage of London churches is the variety of doctrine and ceremony and architecture which they have to offer. All tastes are catered for, and the instinct to worship is strong in all of us. All London churches are open on Sundays, except certain Guild churches in the City. More than half are open on weekdays and daily services are usual in Church of England and Roman Catholic fanes.

Those who recall the London of the 1920s will remember an even richer variety than there is now – the robed last angel sitting on his canopied throne by gaslight in the Catholic Apostolic church in Gordon Square, where people used to speak with tongues. This was before that mighty Gothic Revival fabric (D. and R. Brandon, 1853–5), which looks inside rather like Westminster Abbey without the monuments, was loaned to London University as a chapel. Then there were the Peculiar People from Essex who used to have a mission to London in Lambeth. During the fervent services in their humble building, which was reminiscent of the chapel described in Browning's 'Christmas Eve', one could read their hymn book and find these memorable lines:

> Shall the chapel doors rattle and umbrellas move
> To show that you'll the service disapprove?

The Swedenborgians, supported partly by Mudie's, who ran the famous circulating library, had a Norman Revival church near King's Cross, with a bare table and open Bible. The church of Martin Luther in Hackney was all incense and vestments and its minister could remember when the carriages of rich City merchants crowded the Spelthorne Road.

In the capacious arms of the Church of England, there was even more variety than there is today. Now the tendency is to have a family communion at 9.30, and there is much less distinction between catholic and evangelical worship. Before the war, the City of London had churches

whose incumbents lived as far off as Bexhill and only appeared on Sundays
to take the statutory services. What a joy it was to sit in a box pew while
the gallery clock ticked and to hear the rolling seventeenth-century English
of the Prayer Book alone with the verger and the pew-opener and breathe
in the hassock-scented dust of Dickensian London.

The medieval churches of London are not all that wonderful, if we
except Westminster Abbey. The greatest of them was old St Paul's Cathedral,
then the longest cathedral in Europe. It was so much destroyed in the Fire
that it had to be rebuilt (on a slightly different axis) by Sir Christopher
Wren. The most satisfying architecturally of the early churches of London
is the little Norman chapel of St John in the Tower of London, with its
perfect Romanesque proportions. The next most satisfying with the same
round-arched type is St Bartholomew-the-Great, Smithfield, which is
early twelfth century, but much refurbished by the late Sir Aston Webb at
the end of the last century. It is the choir and Lady Chapel of what once
was a large priory building, and is now famous for its music as well as
its architecture.

As for Westminster Abbey, it is three things. Architecturally, it is a French
medieval cathedral rebuilt by Henry III and belonging to the times when
England and France were one kingdom. It is more like Amiens and Rheims
than an English church. To its east end has been added the amazingly
intricate Tudor chapel of Henry VII, the last and richest flowering of
English flamboyance. Secondly, it is our greatest gallery of monumental
sculpture from the Middle Ages until the Regency. It is thirdly the
embodiment of English history, in stone and glass. It is best enjoyed on a
weekday Evensong in winter, preferably a windy, wet day when there are
not many people about, and when choir and organ scoop out a heaven
from London's central roar. One should sit in a stall in the choir and not
in the nave.

The grandest phase of church building in London was after the Great
Fire of 1666, when Wren was busy on St Paul's and the City churches. He
rebuilt the bodies of the City churches first and added their spires and
towers in Portland stone and lead after he had envisaged the dome of his
cathedral. London must have had the most beautiful skyline in the world
before the Victorians, and more recently modern post-war 'developers',
ruined it with rent-collecting slabs.

No Wren church remains outside as Wren meant you to see it, with
steeple showing above the chimney pots, except for a glimpse of St Martin's,
Ludgate, seen from outside Apothecaries' Hall, Blackfriars, and the tower
and spire of St Mary Abchurch as seen from Sherborne Lane. All else is

blotted out by tall blocks, or stupidly cleared of low buildings from which it was meant to rise, as has been St Lawrence Jewry.

The Victorian and later bishops of London destroyed many of Wren's City churches and the Germans bombed nearly all the rest. Almost all post-war restorations have been spoiled inside by the introduction of stained glass which Wren never intended for his churches. Their colour and decoration was to be in the form of carved wood, plasterwork, and wrought iron and painted altar-piece, with Moses, Aaron, the Commandments and Creed.

St Paul's Cathedral itself is most splendid when viewed floodlit from its west front on a velvet night, or better still from Watling Street at the east end, where the steeple of St Augustine's Church has been restored to Wren's original design by Seely & Paget. Its dark and slender silhouette makes the floodlit white cathedral beyond look colossal. From being impressively blackened, it has been turned by cleaning into the cheerful Renaissance building its architect intended. It now has a smile like that which one sees on the bust of Wren. The interior was spoiled in its proportions in the last century, when the organ screen across the choir was folded back, so that the church does not look as long and mysterious as Wren intended. If there were to be a baldacchino over the high altar, it should have been under the dome and in front of a restored organ screen.

When London City burst its walls in the eighteenth century, and the richer folk started to live in red brick Queen Anne and Georgian squares and mansions in Middlesex and outside the river villages on the Surrey bank, there was much church building in Portland stone. London's three most impressive churches of this time were those by Wren's pupil Nicholas Hawksmoor – Christ Church, Spitalfields (1723–9) locked and awaiting repair (along with the meths drinkers who sit in its churchyard), St George-in-the-East (1715–23), which was bombed hollow and has a smaller new church inside it, and St Anne's, Limehouse (1712–24), also in need of repair, but still open. These three churches sail like clippers over the wharves as one goes downstream to Greenwich.

Equally remarkable on the Surrey bank is London's most splendiferous baroque church, St Paul's, Deptford, by Thomas Archer. Its former rector, the Revd Derek Brown, turned the huge crypt into a boys' club and the grand theatrical interior of his church above is a club for worship. Deptford is now a tough part of London and its people have little official connection with the City and West End.

The other church of this date which everyone knows is St Martin-in-the-Fields (1722–6), by James Gibbs. It was never meant to be seen as it is now, but was designed to rise up from narrow alleys, many of which were in what is now Trafalgar Square. Until Dick Sheppard became its vicar after the First World War, this church looked as though it might become 'redundant'. Now it has become a centre of Christian welfare.

There was a brief, exciting phase of church building at the end of the eighteenth century, which produced some churches with Adam style interiors. The most original is All Hallows', London Wall, by George Dance, Junior (1765–7), with a coved ceiling lit by huge semi-circles and a delicate semi-dome at the east end. This is now largely an exhibition gallery for the Council for the Care of Churches.

London is studded with commissioners' churches which were built to save the new industrial and lower middle classes from atheism after the Napoleonic Wars. Well-known architects of the 1820s were employed, and fixed sums were in many cases given for the building. The idea was to get in as many seats as possible at the lowest cost. The style of the church could be Greek or Gothic.

The three most splendid, on which rather more money than usual was spent, are New St Pancras (1819–22) in the Euston Road, purest Greek without and within, but spoiled inside by inappropriate late Victorian stained glass; St Luke's, Chelsea, by J. Savage (1820–4), in the Gothic style and the first church in London since the Middle Ages to have a stone vault; and St James's, Bermondsey (1829), a classical building by the same architect. The future of this magnificent church seems to be still uncertain.

The most varied, extraordinary, and numerous churches of the metropolis were built by the Victorians. They were put up in the slums and the suburbs, created by steam railways and later by electric tram cars. The old idea of driving atheism out was replaced by the more positive idea of bringing the Gospel to the slums. This was largely the work of Tractarians, the followers of Keble, Pusey and Newman. The last-mentioned went over to Rome. Tractarians who remained loyal to the Church considered that the Catholic Church in this country was Anglican and that the Roman Catholics were the Italian mission. They wanted to build in the slums churches for Catholic ritual which would be uplifting contrasts to their squalid surroundings. They were tall and cathedral-like in proportion and generally built of brick, London's most readily available building material. The west end let in the light; the east end, where the high altar stood, was rich, dark and mysterious.

But then the Victorians 'went on from where Gothic left off' and the most amazing and richly decorated prototype of these is All Saints', Margaret Street, by William Butterfield (1849–59). It is a brick building and inside it is decorated with coloured tiles, since brick does not admit of carving. The decoration becomes richer higher up the walls. In a small confined area it is amazing what a sense of lofty space the architect has created.

The architect G. E. Street, who designed the Law Courts and founded the Arts and Crafts movement by means of his pupil William Morris, built a slightly less high church answer to Butterfield in the brick Lombardo-Gothic masterpiece of St James-the-Less (1858–61) near Victoria Station. Here the proportions inside are broad rather than lofty. In All Saints', Margaret Street, Prebendary Mackay, a former rector, used to say that the stained glass windows reminded him of a good hand at bridge, but the stained glass in St James-the-Less is more like transparent pre-Raphaelite painting, and there is a 'modified doom', that is to say, one with not too much Hell in it, painted by G. F. Watts, over the chancel. Both churches are perfect period pieces, eminently practical and well adapted to high church worship.

The grandest slum churches of this period are undoubtedly the three great brick buildings of St Chad's, Haggerston (1868), by James Brooks and St Columba's, Kingsland Road (1867), by the same architect, and St Augustine's, Kilburn (1870–80), by J. L. Pearson, which is derived from his earlier and fine brick church of St Peter's, Kennington Lane (1863). Brooks went in for height and simplicity with a dark, tall east end and a light nave. Pearson went in for height and stone and brick vaulting and many mysterious vistas and little side chapels. St Augustine's, Kilburn, has the highest spire in London. Dr Pevsner describes it as 'one of the best churches of its date in the whole of England, a proud, honest, upright achievement'.

These churches were all built for Tractarian worship. They are often associated with devoted, gaunt priests, martyred and stoned for ritualism, who strode in their cassocks down dark alleys and by example brought their people to the pleasure of worship and lifted them out of the misery of nineteenth-century industrialism.

There was also the gospel to the richer suburbs, when wives of the wealthy tore off their jewels and gave them to be embroidered into vestments and hammered into altar crosses, and left by will sacred pictures inherited from their families to decorate the church walls. A cathedral of this sort of thing is St Cuthbert's, Philbeach Gardens, in what may now be termed the Australian quarter of London and adjacent to Earls Court Square. It has now a different, though equally live, congregation from that of the 1880s when it was built.

The late Victorians produced more refined and equally original London churches. These were the times when 'artistic' was a favourite word and home handicrafts and folk music were popular, when the *English Hymnal* was better taste than *Hymns Ancient and Modern*, and sermons were more intellectual and less revivalist, and stained glass was greener and paler and pitch and pine gave way to pale oak. Kensington and Chelsea and Ealing each have fine examples of this style. Holy Trinity, Kensington Gore, by G. F. Bodley (1902) is plain and uninviting outside. Inside it is pale green many vista'd twilight hung with mighty chandeliers.

Holy Trinity, Sloane Street (1888–90), by J. D. Sedding, has glass by Burne-Jones, electroliers by Bainbridge Reynolds, carving by Pomeroy and ironwork by Harry Wilson and Nelson Dawson and medallions by Armstead. It is the most elaborate Arts and Crafts church in London. It was built for high church worship but has gone rather low church. To attend Evensong there is to fall back into the world of Pont Street, hansom cabs and Oscar Wilde.

St Jude-on-the-Hill by Sir Edwin Lutyens (1910) and his adjacent free church dominate with their respective steeple and dome the leafy heights of Hampstead Garden Suburb. Inside St Jude's is impressive by its scale and as a repository of Edwardian and later decoration. The little Quaker meeting house by Fred Rowntree near the free church and the flowery lanes and twittens of the suburb make this the most attractive *rus in urbe* in London.

One more of these late Victorian and Edwardian churches, which are plain outside and unexpectedly rich within, must be mentioned. This is the red brick church of St Cyprian, Clarence Gate, by Sir Ninian Comper (1903). A low stone vaulted narthex opens to a wide expanse of polished dark wooden floor in which are reflected slender columns and a lace-like gold screen across the whole width of the church. The daylight is mitigated by bottle glass, the east windows contain Comper's stained glass, and the altars are hung with his rose-pink hangings.

Outside the Church of England, the finest buildings are those of the Roman Catholics. They are all, with the exception of St Ethelreda's, Ely Place, which is much restored medieval, fairly recent. The best of all is the Cathedral of Westminster by J. F. Bentley (1895–1903), in his own Byzantine style: red brick and Portland stone without, marble and yellow London brick within.

The interior is immensely impressive, much more so than is now that of St Paul's. When you are inside St Paul's you expect the dome to look bigger. When you first enter Westminster, you do not expect a central dome at all, until your eye is led by shallow saucer domes, along the nave, to the vast domed central space. The details of the cathedral vary in quality. The earlier chapels at the east end with their mosaics are perfect, and the light fittings are the best anywhere. Bentley and his assistant Marshall, instead of trying to hide electric light as something to be ashamed of, used the naked bulbs as pearls in compositions which are like hanging jewellery.

Brompton Oratory (1878) by H. Gribble is a faithful essay in Italian Baroque and excellent for music and ritual. The Cathedral of St George, Southwark, a rather flimsy building by Pugin in 1841, was bombed, and the present rebuilt structure is most handsomely proportioned in the Gothic style, reminiscent in its loftiness of Maufe's Anglican cathedral of Guildford.

Methodists, Baptists, Congregationalists and others have not built such fine buildings in London as they have in provincial cities. The best are Central Hall, Westminster (1905), by Lanchester and Rickards, Viennese Baroque outside and rather plain, except for its main staircase, within, and the Congregational church, Lyndhurst Road, Hampstead (1833–4), by Alfred Waterhouse, an original hexagonal plan in shiny brick and majolica.

The most historic building in London outside the Christian church is the synagogue (1701) in Bevis Marks off Houndsditch. It is like a City church inside, but spared Victorian accretions. Many eighteenth-century brass candelabra twinkle in a forest of dark woodwork, and you must keep your hat on if you are a man and sit in the gallery if you are a woman.

Part 3

CHURCHES AND CATHEDRALS

'The only bulwark against complete paganism is the church. . . .
It is just because it is so disheartening and so difficult and so easy
to betray, that we must keep this Christian witness going.'

Letter to Evelyn Waugh, Whit Monday 1947

English cathedrals

from *English Cities and Small Towns* (1943)

English cathedrals are, most of them, larger than any other cathedrals in Europe, except St Peter's. They are a memorial of the time when people referred to 'the pious English' and when the square mile of the City of London had over 100 churches. And to this day, the presence of the Church, symbolized by the cathedral, broods over most cathedral towns. From the distance, whether the town is in a valley or on a hill top, the cathedral rides above the houses and draws the landscape round it, flat East Anglian pasture or rounded chalk downs of Wiltshire. When you are in the town itself, the cathedral disappears, though its personality pervades the place in many little churches, some 'low', some 'high', some locked, some bombed, most hidden among shops and winding alleys. Gaitered archdeacons and frequent clergy of less distinctive dress haunt the cathedral cafe, the cathedral bookshop, the chauntrye tea shoppe, the cloister antique shop. Then suddenly at the end of a street or through some monastic gateway to the close you see the cathedral soaring into the sky. At once it is bigger, more majestic, more richly textured than you would have believed possible. And in the silence of the close, where ilex, lilac and copper beech hang over walled gardens of the canons' houses and where gigantic elms rise from smooth stretches of emerald grass, the cathedral is so vast and so old, so unbelievable a piece of engineering in the poise and counterpoise of local stone that you feel you must whisper, if you want to speak at all, even outside it.

Here in another country my mind goes to Salisbury, my favourite cathedral city. There is the usual wide market square of a county town, mellow brick houses and a quantity of inns, some small beer houses for thirsty drovers, some jazzed-up hostelryes for motorists; there is St Thomas's church, of pale grey stone among the red tiles and brick, with its slender fifteenth-century interior; the main streets whose multiple stores have left fairly unharmed the old buildings above the shop fronts; the long grey wall of the cathedral precincts; and then that huge, silent, tree-shadowed close, acres of retreating grass as a setting for the vertical lines of the great cathedral with its tremendous spire nearly as high as the distant downs.

And if the interior of Salisbury is now a little cold, stripped of its wall painting and ancient glass, I think of Winchester, that endless nave where screen and transept and aisle suggest, by branching roof and intersecting vaults, vista upon vista beyond to God himself. Or I remember an Evensong at Hereford, a remote cathedral less visited than many, where I was one of a small congregation listening to the contemplative service of Evensong which had been kept up through the Reformation and the centuries; the well-trained choir from the choir school, the tenors and basses and altos from the town: the psalms: a canon reading the lesson, appearing from the dark recess of a stall: the intoned prayers and the 'Amen' floating up to the vaulting: the sweet Victorian anthem in tune with Sir Gilbert Scott's pious restoration of the fabric. Or I am back at a Three Choirs Festival in Gloucester, hearing Handel among the heavy Norman pillars of the nave and glimpsing, beyond, that lace-like miracle of glass and stone; the choir at Gloucester where England first bred the Perpendicular style, the last and, to me, most beautiful phase of Gothic. Or I am saying my last prayers in England, before leaving for Ireland, in the early light shining on pink sandstone in Chester Cathedral, a square and strong and northern looking building. Or I am rowing on the river at Ely and glancing up at the cathedral on the slope above me, the ingenious lantern at the intersection of nave transepts and choir, the stately towers at the west, the aisles and chapels bursting out from the masonry into rich churches of their own. Three other cathedral memories remain: being shown round Canterbury at midnight by the light of an electric torch on Norman capital and distant vault and finally there at my feet a circle of light on the spot where St Thomas à Becket was murdered: standing in the whispering gallery of St Paul's as the shadows grew down the empty nave on the night of one of the heaviest raids on the City when a time bomb fell into St Paul's churchyard and did not explode: a fine September evening in that first most sinister year of the War, when the youth fellowship of my home village was having its final fling, a day's outing by char-a-banc to Cheddar Gorge; the bishop showed us round the moated palace at Wells and from the palace garden we looked across to the east end of the cathedral where the late light cast long shadows on the golden Somerset stone. I remember thinking then that I must store in my mind every detail, the flowers in the palace garden, the fishponds, the sculptured proportions of that kind country cathedral, for here was the heart of England, and an unforgettable monument of Christendom.

However you see them, whether for a service, or for a moment in the close, or for a gaping, guide-conducted tour, the cathedrals dwarf the towns and cities where they are. When you are out again in the streets, shops and war and factories and buses and trams are trivial and unimportant. In some places, the town has become industrialized and eaten its way almost to the cathedral gates as at Chester, Gloucester, Durham and Worcester, or it has hardly grown at all as at Ely and Wells; or it has become noisy and crowded, too narrow and old for all the traffic which has been allowed by a careless generation to pour into it, as at Chichester, York, Winchester, Salisbury and St Albans: whatever has happened, the cathedral still rules. Loud over the internal combustion engine sound its bells, even if, for the present, they only strike the hour.

St Protus and St Hyacinth, Blisland, Cornwall

BBC Radio, 21 July 1948

Down what lanes, across how many farmyards, resting in how many valleys, topping what hills and suddenly appearing round the corners of what ancient city streets are the churches of England? The many pinnacles in Somerset, of rough granite from the moors in Devon and Cornwall, of slate by the sea coasts, brushed with lichen, spotted with saffron, their rings of five and six bells pouring music among the windy elm trees as they have poured their sound for centuries, still they stand, the towers and spires of the West.

They are still there as in the days when villagers still came to church and when footpaths were still left by farmers. There are about 20,000 churches in England and of these quite a half are ancient. They are more in number than one could see in a lifetime. I have seen about 5,000 and I hope I shall be spared to see as many more.

I know no greater pleasure than church-crawling. You never know what you are going to find: an eccentric incumbent, a derelict church, a live church, an ugly or a lovely one, or just a church. And even if it's 'just a church', there is always something about it for those who have eyes and ears and imagination. Oh, if you have not taken to it yet, let me advise the hobby of church-crawling! It is the richest of pleasures: it leads you to the remotest and quietest country, it introduces you to the history of England in stone and wood and glass, which is always truer than what you read in books. You meet all sorts of people on your travels. You learn to know where to find the key: to look under the mat, in the lantern of the porch, under the porch roof, behind the notice board, or to enquire at the nearest cottage – or perhaps it will mean a long bicycle ride to the parsonage.

In the days when food was plentiful, what teas I have enjoyed on rectory and vicarage lawns, what talks in book-lined studies, what friends I have made – and all because of church-crawling.

Some learn their faith from books, some from relations, some (a very few) learn it at school. I learned mine from church-crawling. Indeed it was through looking at churches that I came to believe in the reason why churches were built and why, despite neglect and contempt, innovation and business bishops, they still survive and continue to grow and prosper, especially in our industrial towns.

I'm afraid I'm like Sir Walter Scott (but not so good a writer): I take a long time getting to the point. This series of talks is about three West Country churches and this one is about Blisland in Cornwall. I must remember that. But I'm not ready to start yet. You must have the instruments of the church-crawler. The first of these is a map. A one-inch Ordnance map: no others will do. That map tells you whether the church has a tower or spire, for it is marked with a cross and black square if it's a tower, a black circle if it's a spire. Then you can generally assume that a country church is old, even if it has no tower or spire, if the map shows the dotted lines of footpaths leading to it.

The next thing you need is an eye. Please notice that. An *eye*. Not knowledge of style of architectures, of squinches, squints, piscinae, aumbries and all the other jargon of the church guidebooks. Look at the church for what it is: a place of worship and a piece of architecture combined. You will read much nonsense in many guidebooks. They will tell you that something is in the 'debased' style, meaning that it was built in the sixteenth, seventeenth or eighteenth centuries. But it does not matter when it was built or whether it is 'pure' or 'debased'. What does matter is: do you like the look of it yourself? Instead of bothering about dates and what the guidebooks say is old, use your own eyes. Something is not beautiful simply because it is old. But it is more likely to be than not, for there is no doubt that most of what is modern, especially in the way of church furniture, is ugly. We have emerged out of civilization into barbarism, so naturally we have a few barbaric objects to commemorate the times we live in – the gimcrack rubbish in 'children's corners'. (I always remember that story of a caustic old clergyman in Oxford who was asked what he thought was the best furnishing for a children's corner. 'A birch rod,' he replied.) Then there is that awful combination of unstained oak and powder-blue hangings so popular for side altars. There are the hideous floodlighting schemes, the mutton-fisted electric-light fixtures. Ideally, no old church should have electric lights at all: their glare is too harsh for the delicate texture of an old building. Candles are the best light of all or, failing that, oil lamps; and if it must be electric lights, as many bulbs as possible of the lowest power possible.

And now for Blisland. Of all the country churches of the West I have seen, I think it is the most beautiful. I was a boy when I first saw it, 30 or more years ago. I shall never forget that first visit – bicycling to the inland and unvisited parts of Cornwall from my home by the sea. The trees at home were few and thin, sliced and leaning away from the fierce Atlantic gales. The walls of the high Cornish hedges were made of slate stuffed in between with fern and stonecrop and the pulpy green triangles of mesembryanthemum, sea vegetation of a windy sea-coast country. On a morning after a storm, you might find the blown yellow spume from Atlantic rollers lying trembling in the wind on inland fields. Then, as huge hill followed huge hill and I sweated as I pushed my bicycle up and heart in mouth went swirling down into the next valley, the hedges became higher, the lanes ran down ravines, the plants seemed lusher, the thin Cornish elms seemed bigger and the slate houses and slate hedges gave place to granite ones. I was on the edge of Bodmin Moor, that sweet brown home of Celtic saints, that haunted, thrilling land so full of ghosts of ancient peoples whose hut circles, beehive dwellings and burial mounds jut out above the ling and heather. Great wooded valleys, white below the tree trunks with wood anemones or blue with bluebells, form a border fence on this, the western side of Bodmin Moor.

Perched on the hill above the wood stands Blisland village. It has not one ugly building in it and what is unusual in Cornwall, the houses are round a green. Between the lichen-crusted trunks of elm and ash that grow on the green, you can see everywhere the beautiful silver-grey moorland granite. It is used for windows, for chimney stacks, for walls. One old house has gable ends (sixteenth or seventeenth century, I should think) carved in it, which curl round like Swiss rolls. The church is down a steep slope of a graveyard, past slate headstones, and looks over the treetops of a deep and elmy valley and away and away to the west where, like a silver shield, the Atlantic sometimes shines in the sun. An opening in the churchyard circle shows a fuchsia hedge and the vicarage front door beyond. The tower is square and weathered and made of enormous blocks of this moorland granite, each block as big as a chest of drawers. However did those old masons haul them up to the topmost stages? When I first saw it, the tower was stuffed with moss and with plants that had rooted there between the great stones. But lately it has been most vilely repointed in hard straight lines with cement. And the church itself, which seems to lean this way and that, throws out chapels and aisles in all directions. It hangs on the hillside, spotted with lichens that have even softened the slates of its roof. Granite forms the tracery of its windows; a granite holy-water spout meets you in the porch.

The whitewashed porch, the flapping notices, the door! That first thrill of turning the handle of the door of a church never seen before, or a church dearly loved and visited again and again like Blisland – who but the confirmed church-crawler knows it?

The greatest living church architect, Mr J. N. Comper, says a church should bring you to your knees when first you enter it. Such a church is Blisland. For there, before me as I open the door, is the blue-grey granite arcade, that hardest of stones to carve. One column slopes outwards as though it was going to tumble down the hill and its carved wooden beam is fixed between it and the south wall to stop it falling. The floor is of blue slate and pale stone. Old carved benches of dark oak and a few chairs are the seating. The walls are white, the sun streams in through a clear west window, and there – glory of glories! – right across the whole eastern end of the church is a richly painted screen. It is of wood. The panels at its base are red and green. Wooden columns highly coloured, twisted like barley sugar, burst into gilded tracery and fountain out to hold a panelled rood loft. There are steps in the wall to reach it. Our Lord and His Mother and St John, who form the rood, are over the centre of the screen. My eyes look up and there is the irregular old Cornish roof, shaped like the inside of an upturned ship, all its ribs richly carved, the carving shown up by white plaster panels. These old roofs, beautifully restored, are to be seen throughout the whole church, stretching away beyond the cross, down the aisles. I venture in a little further. There, through this rich screen, I can mark the blazing gold of the altars and the medieval-style glass, some of the earliest work of Comper. And here beside me in the nave is a pulpit shaped like a wineglass, in the Georgian style and encrusted with cherubs and fruit carved in wood.

I think I said when I started this talk that all you needed was an eye to see, not a knowledge of dates and history. That screen, the glory of this church, the golden altars, the stained glass and the pulpit are comparatively new. They were designed by F. C. Eden in 1897 and he died only a year or two ago. Mr Eden had a vision of this old Cornish church as it was in medieval times. He did not do all the medieval things he might have done. He did not paint the walls with pictures of angels, saints and devils in amber and red, and he left the western windows clear that people in this reading age might see their books. He put in a Georgian pulpit. He centred everything on the altar, to which the screen is, as it were, a golden, red and green veil to the holiest mystery behind it.

Now what does it matter about dates and styles in Blisland church? There is Norman work in it and there is fifteenth- and sixteenth-century work and there is sensitivity and beautiful modern work. But chiefly it is a living church whose beauty makes you gasp, whose silence brings you to your knees, even if you kneel on the hard stone and slate of the floor, worn smooth by generations of worshippers.

The valley below the church was hot and warm when first I saw this granite-cool interior. Valerian sprouted on the vicarage wall. A castor-oil tree traced its leaves against a western window. Grasshoppers and birds chirruped. St Protus and St Hyacinth, patron saints of Blisland church, pray for me! Often in a bus or train I call to mind your lovely church, the stillness of that Cornish valley and the first really beautiful work of man that my boyhood vividly remembers.

St Mark's, Swindon, Wiltshire

BBC Radio, 4 August 1948

The train draws into the outskirts of a big town. There they are, pricking the skyline above suburban chimney pots, the spires and towers of Victorian churches. Clean-looking in seaside towns, smoke-blackened in industrial ones. Sometimes no spire or tower at all but a red-brick affair with a huge roof, built in the 1880s, bombed in the 1940s. Tinkle-tinkle in the early morning, the little billcote at the west end calls the faithful few to a week-day service – to the dark but half-repaired interior of a chapel of ease. One-two-three! Four-five-six! Over the housetops rings that lush, sweet-toned peal from St Luke's or St Mark's or St Michael and All Angels – the favourite saints' names for Victorian churches. One-two-three! Four-five-six! Softly the organist starts the voluntary; bright gleams the gas on tiles and shiny pews; ruby red and topaz and blue stained-glass windows inter-rupt an evening twilight; and when the bells are down the surpliced choir moves into the chancel to the strains of Ellerton's 'The Day-ay Thou Gavest, Lord, is Ended'.

So were the Victorian churches of our youth. So are they today except that some have, alas, been floodlit and some are bombed – forming far more picturesque ruins than many an older building – and almost all are despised as architecture except by the discriminating few, among whom are you who listen to me tonight. For who, who doesn't know it, wants to hear of St Mark's, Swindon? Swindon is no beauty spot. St Mark's is not even the old parish church. It is not even an outstanding example, as Victorian churches go. But it is a famous church and a live one. I have chosen it because it calls to mind two things about English churches that I have not yet mentioned: Victorian architecture and parish life.

So forgive me for a moment while I take you on a church crawl round other Victorian churches of the West. Everybody is so busy running down the Victorians or laughing at them that this is a chance to speak up in their favour. 'Ha! Ha!' says the vicar when I go to get the key. 'You can't want to see *our* church. It's a Victorian monstrosity, my dear fellow,' and he gives me a look that suggests that I really want the key in order to burgle the offertory box. 'But I think your church is *beautiful*,' I say. And he thinks I'm mad. Ah, vicars who despise Victorian churches, church-wardens with 'artistic' leanings, advisory boards and art critics: listen a while to the praise of some West Country Victorians, and then we'll go back to Swindon and St Mark's.

Let's admit straightaway that when they were restoring old buildings even the greatest Victorian architects were arrogant, heavy-handed and insensitive to all but some phase of Gothic architecture of which they approved. Cornish people will not willingly forgive Mr J. P. St Aubyn for his workmanlike but hideous 'restoration' of most Cornish churches. His signature tune is an iron foot-scraper by the porch. If you see that foot-scraper, you know J. P. St Aubyn has been at the church and there will not be much that's old left inside the building.

But when they were starting from scratch, Victorian church architects were often as original and creative and as beautiful as any who have built before or since them. George Edmund Street, that indefatigable bearded genius who died in 1881 from overwork on building the law courts of London – George Edmund Street was a brilliant artist, a scholarly and entertaining writer and the inspiring master of William Morris, Philip Webb, Norman Shaw and J. D. Sedding. Life in his office was fun. One of his pupils had a stutter and could only sing without stuttering, and so Morris and Webb and Shaw used to talk to him in Gregorian plainsong through rolled-up tubes of drawing paper. George Edmund Street designed St John's, Torquay, in 1867, for which Burne-Jones later did some pictures. He designed Holy Trinity, Barnstaple, and All Saints', Clifton, and in 1874 the superb church of Kingston in Dorset, which sits so stately on a hill slope and gleams with Purbeck marble.

All Street's churches are built on rigid principles. These are they: plenty of light from the west so that people can see their books; local materials; no screen; the altar visible from all parts of the church; and every detail down to the door hinges specially designed and very practical. One of his last works was the splendid nave of Bristol Cathedral. Then Street's pupil J. D. Sedding designed that noble clean and soaring church of All Saints, Falmouth, in 1887.

Perhaps the most amazing church in Devon was that designed by Butterfield at Yealmpton in 1850 – a mass of local marbles like that original font he made for Ottery St Mary. Other great Victorian churches of the West are Truro Cathedral and St Stephen's, Bournemouth, by J. L. Pearson – tall buildings these, with infinite vistas of vaulted arches cutting vaulted arches. Pearson was a vista man – vistas and variety. And I have always had a weakness for that late-Victorian church St David's at Exeter by W. D. Caroe. A pale green building it is, with all sorts of funny quirks in the way of stone tracery and woodwork and metal – a sort of ecclesiastical vision of the old Deller's Cafe of Exeter.

Then there are Victorian churches that later architects have made more beautiful, like All Saints', Clevedon, and Wimborne St Giles in Dorset. One more I must mention before I move on to St Mark's is an Edwardian affair built for Lord Beauchamp by A. Randall Wells – the new church of Kempley in Gloucestershire. It is a sturdy little thing in stone with an extraordinary and enormous west window whose tracery is just a large diamond pattern in stone. This place inside is a miniature cathedral of the Arts and Crafts movement: local labour was employed on it. Edward Burnsley, the Cotswold cabinetmaker, made the lectern, that fine craftsman Ernest Garrison made the candlesticks, and the last surviving carver of figureheads for the old clippers carved the figures of Our Lord, St Mary and St John on the beam. The woodwork itself in the church was painted by villagers in vermilion, ruby, golden ochre, yellow, chrome green and blue. From Yealmpton to Kempley, these churches of another generation are arresting in the extreme. They are not copies of medieval: they are thinking in Gothic. They are original, violent, surprising. They take some getting used to. But they are full of thought and care and were inspired by the faith of their architects and builders. There's nothing tame or mediocre about them. Do go and have a look at some of those I have mentioned, if you happen to be near them.

Now for parish life. The train draws into the outskirts of a big town. It is Swindon. One hundred and eight years ago there was nothing here at all but a canal and a place where two newly built railways joined, the Cheltenham & Great West Union Railway (the Gloucestershire line) and the London to Bristol line, known as the Great Western and which not rack nor thumbscrew will ever induce me to call 'Western Region British Railways'. On a hill above the meadow was the old market town of Swindon. Then New Swindon was built in the meadow by the Great Western. It was a convenient point between Bristol and London. It consisted of sheds and a few rows of model cottages with open fields round them. These cottages are of Bath stone taken from the excavations of Box Tunnel. They still exist and are called the Company's Houses. They must form one of the earliest planned industrial estates in Britain.

The parishioners of St Philip and St Jacob in Bristol entreated the Great Western to build a church for their workers. Directors stumped up money, subscriptions were raised, land was presented and by 1845 St Mark's Church was built.

There it stands today, close beside the line on the Bristol side of the station – a stone building, all spikes and prickles outside, designed by Sir George Gilbert Scott who was then a young man and who lived to build St Pancras Hotel and the Foreign Office in London and to 'restore' many cathedrals. (I have written 'restore' in inverted commas. I hope you can hear them.) One cannot call it a convenient site. Whistles and passing trains disturb the service; engine smoke blackens the leaves and tomb-stones and eats into the carved stonework of the steeple. No matter: it is a great church and though it isn't much to look at, it is for me the greatest church in England. For not carved stones nor screens and beautiful altars nor lofty cascades nor gilded canopies but the priests who minister and the people who worship make a church great. If ever I feel England is pagan, if ever I feel the poor old C. of E. is tottering to its grave, I revisit St Mark's, Swindon. That corrects the impression at once. A simple and infinite faith is taught: St Mark's and its daughter churches are crowded. Swindon, so ugly to look at to the eyes of the architectural student, glows golden as the New Jerusalem to eyes that look beyond the brick and stone.

For there's no doubt that Swindon *is* superficially ugly. That pretty model village of the 1840s has developed a red-brick rash that stretches up to the hill to Old Swindon and strangles it, and beyond Old Swindon it runs tentacles to the downs and it spreads with monotony in all other directions. It is now the biggest town in Wiltshire, 60 times the size of the original market town. But I would rather see a red-brick rash (and mind you, Swindon has few if any slums; it is only ugly architecturally) – I would rather see a red-brick rash like Swindon enlivened with Victorian towers and steeples sticking out of it than I would see a gleaming glass city of architect-designed flats with never a church but instead only the humped backs of super-cinemas, the grandstands of greyhound tracks and the bubbling cocoa fountains of community workers – all these cathedrals of the modern barbarism.

For Swindon is largely a Christian town and much of the credit for that goes to the priests and people of St Mark's. It is not Sabbatarian and smug. It has its cinemas and theatres and an art gallery and library and sports grounds and good old Swindon Town Football Club – but its churches are part of its life. That is the unusual thing about Swindon. In the cen-tenary book of St Mark's, which appeared in 1945, there is a photograph of Canon Ponsonby wearing side whiskers and a beard that ran under his chin but not over it. This saintly Victorian priest (who died in 1945 aged nearly 100) caused St Mark's parish so to grow in faith that it built five other churches in New Swindon. Two of them, St Paul's and St Augustine's, became separate parishes. He also caused the Wantage Sisters to open their mission house in Swindon. The work went on under the famous Canon Ross, his successor, and continues with the present vicar, through whom the beautiful daughter church of St Mark's was built, called St Luke's. It was designed by W. A. Masters. I can safely say that, except for the railway works, which are awe-inspiring inside, St Luke's is the only fine interior, architecturally, in Swindon.

But it's not about lovely St Luke's nor about little St John's nor about the missions that St Mark's supports abroad nor about the many priests who have been Swindon men that I want to end this talk. Up a steep hill going out of the New Town winds Old Swindon. There is a church built of wood and called St Saviour's. That was erected in 1889–90 in six months by St Mark's men, mostly railway workers. When you consider that they did this in their spare time and for nothing, that some of them sacrificed their holidays and that their working hours were from 6 a.m. to 5.30 p.m. in those days, you can imagine the faith that inspired them to go out after a long day's work and build a church. Of course, with foundations of faith like this, St Saviour's grew and in 1904 it had to be enlarged. Over a hundred men once again set to work and the church was extended entirely by voluntary labour and in spare time.

I don't know why it is that St Mark's parish hangs together and is a living community, full of life and spirit. Perhaps it is because Swindon is the right size for an industrial town, neither too big nor too small. Perhaps it is because of the sort of work men do in a railway works – 'inside' as they call it in Swindon. Perhaps it's because the men 'inside' do not do soul-destroying work such as one sees in motor factories where the ghastly chain-belt system persists. Perhaps much of the work in a railway works is really worth doing and not beneath the dignity of man. But whatever it is, I know that the people of Swindon first taught me not to be so la-di-da and architectural, not to judge people by the houses they live in, nor churches only by their architecture. I would sooner be on my knees with-in the wooden walls of St Saviour's than leaning elegantly forward in a cushioned pew in an Oxford college chapel – that is to say, if I am to realize there is something beyond this world worth thinking about.

The church-crawler starts by liking *old* churches but ends by liking all churches, and of all churches those that are most alive are often those hard-looking buildings founded by Victorian piety – churches like St Mark's, Swindon.

St Endellion

BBC Radio, 1 July 1949

Saint Endellion! Saint Endellion! The name is like a ring of bells. I travelled late one summer evening to Cornwall in a motor car. The road was growing familiar, Delabole with its slate quarry passed, then Pendogget. Gateways in the high fern-stuffed hedges showed sudden glimpses of the sea. Port Isaac Bay with its sweep of shadowy cliffs stretched all along to Tintagel. The wrinkled Atlantic Ocean had the evening light upon it. The stone and granite manor house of Tresungers with its tower and battlements was tucked away out of the wind on the slope of a valley, and there on the top of the hill was the old church of St Endellion. It looked, and still looks, just like a hare. The ears are the pinnacles of the tower and the rest of the hare, the church, crouches among wind-slashed firs.

On that evening the light bells with their sweet tone were being rung for practice. There's a ringer's rhyme in the tower, painted on a board. It shows Georgian ringers in knee breeches and underneath is written a rhyme which ends with these fine four lines:

> Let's all in love and Friendship hither come
> Whilst the shrill treble calls to thundering Tom
> And since bells are for modest recreation
> Let's rise and ring and fall to admiration.

They were ringing rounds on all six bells. But as we drew near the tower – a grand, granite, fifteenth-century tower looking across half Cornwall as we climbed the hill – the bells sounded louder even than the car. 'St Endellion! St Endellion!' they seemed to say. 'St Endellion!' Their music was scattered from the rough lichened openings over foxgloves, over grey slate roofs, lonely farms and feathery tamarisks, down to that cluster of whitewashed houses known as Trelights, the only village in the parish, and to Roscarrock and Trehaverock and Trefreock, heard perhaps, if the wind was right where lanes run steep and narrow to that ruined, forgotten fishing place of Port Quin, 'St Endellion!' It was a welcome to Cornwall, and in front of us the sun was setting over Gulland and making the Atlantic at Polzeath and Pentire glow like a copper shield.

Ora pro nobis Sancta Endelienta! The words are carved in strangely effective lettering on two of the new oak benches in the church. Incidentally, those carved benches, which incorporate some of the old Tudor ones, are very decent-looking for modern pews. They were designed by the present rector and carved by a local sculptress. But who was St Endellion? She was a sixth-century Celtic saint, daughter of a Welsh king, who with her sisters Minver and Teath and many other holy relations came to North Cornwall with the gospel.

There was an Elizabethan writer who lived in the parish, Nicholas Roscarrock. He loved the old religion and was imprisoned in the Tower and put on the rack and then imprisoned again. He wrote the life of his parish saint. 'St Endelient' he called her and said she lived only on the milk of a cow: 'which cowe the lord of Trenteny kild as she strayed into his grounds; and as olde people speaking by tradition, doe report, she had a great man to her godfather, which they also say was King Arthure, whoe took the killing of the cowe in such sort, as he killed or caus'd the Man to be slaine, whom she miraculously revived.' Nicholas Roscarrock also wrote a hymn in her praise:

> To emitate in part thy vertues rare
> Thy Faith, Hope, Charitie, thy humble mynde,
> Thy chasteness, meekness, and thy dyet spare
> And that which in this Worlde is hard to finde
> The love which thou to enemye didst showe
> Reviving him who sought thy overthrowe.

When she was dying Endelient asked her friends to lay her dead body on a sledge and to bury her where certain young Scots bullocks or calves of a year old should of their own accord draw her. This they did and the Scots bullocks drew the body up to the windy hilltop where the church now stands.

The churchyard is a forest of upright Delabole slate headstones, a rich grey-blue stone, inscribed with epitaphs – the art of engraving lettering on slate continued in this district into the present century – names and rhymes set out on the stone spaciously, letters delicate and beautiful. From the outside it's the usual Cornish church – a long low building of elvan stone, most of it built in Tudor times. But the tower is extra special. It is of huge blocks of granite brought, they say, from Lundy Island. The ground stage of the tower is strongly moulded but the builders seem to have grown tired and to have taken less trouble with the detail higher up, though the blocks of granite are still enormous.

I can remember Endellion before its present restoration. There's a photograph of what it used to look like in the porch – pitch pine pews, pitch pine pulpit, swamping with their yellow shine the clustered granite columns of the aisles. Be careful as you open the door not to fall over. Three steps *down* and there it is, long and wide and light and simple with no pitch pine anywhere except a lectern. A nave and two aisles with barrel roofs carved with bosses, some of them old but most of them done 12 years ago by a local joiner, the village postman and the sculptress. The floor is slate. The walls are stone lightly plastered blueish-grey. There is no stained glass. Old oak and new oak benches, strong and firm and simple, fill, but do not crowd, the church. They do not hide the full length of these granite columns. The high altar is long and vast. At the end of the south aisle is the sculptured base of St Endelienta's shrine, in a blue-black slate called Cataclewse, a boxwood among stones. The church reveals itself at once. Though at first glance it is unmysterious, its mystery grows. It is the mystery of satisfying proportion – and no, not just that, nor yet the feeling of age, for the present church is almost wholly early Tudor, not very old as churches go, nor is the loving use of local materials all to do with it. Why does St Endellion seem to go on praying when there is no one in it? The Blessed Sacrament is not reserved here, yet the building is alive.

There is something strange and exalting about this windy Cornish hilltop looking over miles of distant cliffs, that cannot be put into words.

Down a path from the north door, bordered with fuchsias, is the rectory. The rector of St Endellion is also a prebendary. This church is run by a college of priests like St George's Chapel, Windsor. There are four prebends in the college, though their building is gone and they live elsewhere. They are the prebends of Marny, Trehaverock, Endellion and Bodmin. Each of the prebendal stalls has a little income attached to it and is held by local priests. The money is given to Christian causes. For instance, the parish of Port Isaac, formed out of St Endellion in 1913, is financed with the income of the Bodmin prebendary. How this heavenly medieval arrangement of a college of prebendary clergymen survived the Reformation and Commonwealth and Victorian interferers is another mystery of St Endellion for which we must thank God. It was certainly saved from extinction by the late Athelstan Riley and Lord Clifden. Episcopal attacks have been made on it; but long live St Endellion, Trehaverock, Marny and Bodmin! Hold fast. *Sancta Endelienta, ora pro nobis!*

The rectors of St Endellion have long been remarkable men. There was Parson Hocken, a blacksmith's son from St Teath, who grew roses, was a

Tractarian of the Parson Hawker type, and when jeered at for his lowly origin hung a blacksmith's shoe over his pulpit and preached about it. There was Parson Josa, whom I just remember, who started as a choirboy in St Peter's, Rome, and then joined our own Church of England; there is the present rector, Prebendary Murphy, a joiner and scientist and, above all, a sound theologian. I can safely say, as an experienced sermon-taster of over 40 summers, that he is the most interesting and sensible preacher I have heard. But sermons are not everything as all the rectors of St Endellion have known.

I take a last look at St Endellion standing on a cliff top of this Atlantic coast. The sun turns the water into moving green. In November weather, if the day is bright, the cliffs here are in shadow. The sun cannot rise high enough to strike them. The bracken is dead and brown, the grassy cliff tops vivid green; red berries glow in bushes. Ice-cream cartons and cigarette packets left by summer visitors have been blown into crevices and soaked to pulp. The visitors are there for a season. Man's life on earth will last for 70 years perhaps. But this sea will go on swirling against these green and purple rocks for centuries. Long after we are dead it will rush up in waterfalls of whiteness that seem to hang halfway up the cliff face and then come pouring down with tons of ginger-beery foam. Yet compared with the age of these rocks, the sea's life is nothing. And even the age of rocks is nothing compared with the eternal life of man. And up there on the hill in St Endellion Church, eternal man comes week by week in the Eucharist. That is the supreme mystery of all the mysteries of St Endellion.

Tercentenary of Staunton Harold church, Leicestershire

BBC Radio, 30 December 1953

Everything that I'm saying is apparently going to be put down on gramophone records for the wireless, and it fills one with additional humiliation because it really is a humbling honour to come here this afternoon. It's humbling for me, and for us all in one way, because of the great beauty of this church in which we are and because of the beautiful day it is outside and the beautiful house and park and lake in this gentle part of Leicestershire.

It's humbling to me in particular because I'm a complete stranger to this district, and in self-defence I ought to say that when I was asked to talk I said: 'Do get somebody who really knows about it.' And they said: 'Oh, no. You're just the man.' And so do forgive any ignorance that I may show of your district; I've never been here before in my life until today and now that I am here I really wish I'd been here all my life, for the atmosphere is something we can't put into words and it's here in this church and it's all round this – one might say – *holy* park. There's only one place that I know that's something like it: where I live in Wantage in Berkshire, which is incidentally the county from which Archbishop Laud came, whose vestments are part of the frontal here. In Wantage, in the convent there of our own Church of England's sisters, the Community of St Mary the Virgin, there's an atmosphere there of prayer that one has got here. It's most extraordinary: you must have noticed it in the service – one notices it as one comes into those gates; its people have prayed here in the past and are praying now and it's part of the great Church of England that has gone on through the centuries – not just the three that this church has been built but hundreds and hundreds of years before.

And another humbling thing that I have to open with is that there are many here very much more learned than I. I can see some of them in these beautiful pews. I can see on my left, if I look, Mr Burrow who was chaplain here and who wrote a paper about this church that really tells you everything about it – far more thoroughly and more interestingly than I can do it. But since I am here, put up with all that self-pity and I will start.

The architecture: I'm putting it first though it isn't as important as some of the other things. It is, you notice, in stone. This is a Gothic church and it's what we call in the guidebooks 'Perp' – Perpendicular. I suppose that the tracery there is rather Early Perp – almost 'Decorated'; so is the tracery there; so is the east window. The clerestory is clearly Perp with the perpendicular lines characteristic of that last phase of medieval Gothic and the arcading and the arches and this arch here above my head and those arches there – they're all Perpendicular. And so is the tower outside, such as you would see on any hilltop in Leicestershire or indeed in Derbyshire. They seem to build the churches on the tops of the hills, but here we are in a valley. So it's a country church like other Derbyshire and Leicestershire churches, but built in a Leicestershire valley. I wonder if it was built in a valley because it was the only one to be built at the time; for, as you know, this is the only large church in the country to have been built during the time of Oliver Cromwell when you weren't allowed to build churches. I take Cromwell to be a detestable man. Personally he may have been all right but Puritanism is to me the end of everything: I mean it's everything that one hates – or at least, that *I* do. I say, I must be careful.

And this is not Puritan, I'm happy to say, and indeed it expresses the Church of England which is both catholic and reformed. And this church you're in seems deliberately to have been built as a Gothic church – but then they said: It is reformed and it is catholic and we're going to make it beautiful in the way of the prayer book worship; and they've built a sort of heraldic arch by which you've all come in here under the tower, and you'll notice that this is a kind of warning of what you're to expect inside. Not the Gothic church that this stone architecture would lead you to expect but something different.

Now, let's suppose, just for a minute, that this church were really a medieval church and not a most extraordinary thing – a church built in 1655 in the style of 1455. Let us imagine it was really built in 1455: what would you see? A cross where I'm standing, a wooden screen, above it a loft, all beautifully painted and gilded; above that a rood – that is to say, the figure of Our Lord on the Cross, Our Lady and St John on either side; the walls plastered as now and all covered with paintings of saints – a picture of St Christopher where you could most easily see it as you came in at the door (which would not be at the west end but probably there at the south side and possibly one at the north); and the altar, ablaze with jewels but scarcely visible because of the screen. There might also have been side chapels there and there and partly screens around them for chantry priests; and there wouldn't have been any pews, or if there were any they would have been low wooden benches and very few of them, and the weakest went to the wall, as you know, and would sit along around the edge of the wall.

That's what it would probably have been like: a mass of colour and the people rather noisy and smelly in the nave; the priests, when they were saying the services which you could hardly hear, hidden behind the screens. A superstitious sort of worship – but there's nothing wrong with a little superstition; I rather wish there were more nowadays (I mean more reverent superstition and less astrology). But it *was* a superstitious sort of worship. And then we've got this new but old church, its worship based on the prayer book – our beloved prayer book – and bringing out its catholic meaning as well as getting rid of the abuses that occurred when it was all very dim and vague behind screens. You've got pews for people to sit in, a pulpit that is far more prominent than the medieval pulpit would have been, and a desk for the clerk to read from. The altar is visible – though not wholly visible when these gates are shut: a little mystery is allowed and that is the beauty of a screen, that it doesn't make everything too obvious.

And I must just now pause for a moment and do a little bit of technical stuff and read my notes because – yes. One further thing before I go into the subject of Elizabethan worship. The nave is where people were, the chancel for the priests, and it's symbolized in this church in the roof. If you look up, there is the creation, the world coming out of chaos: I imagine that's what it is. There's the New Testament Greek and here's the Old Testament Hebrew name for God, the latter mis-done, I believe. According to the scholars they've got it all wrong, haven't they? Yes, but that's what they meant, isn't it? Yes, Jehovah there said, That's the world. Here are the angels singing in Heaven – Heaven in the chancel where God is, in the sacraments. The people here in the nave have the world above them – the sun and moon – just the same as the medieval idea. Here is the screen, cutting you off but not entirely from the most sacred, the most wonderful thing that can happen to any of us, when we are present at Holy Communion and the bread and wine are consecrated – something there have been arguments about for years and that there will never be an end to and nobody will have the last word to say. We'll know in Heaven what the answer to that is. Meanwhile, one thing we do know who are Christians: that there's a world of angels and spirits all round us and that at Holy Communion, in some way, we receive everlasting life. And that's symbolized in this church very clearly, emphasized in our prayer book, and this architecture is all designed to emphasize that.

Now its style for one moment. Those pews you're sitting in, that panelling all round the walls and round the arcades, this panelling here, especially the lower part of it is all, I should say, 1655; so is the beautiful organ screen – that is, Renaissance in style – unknown in a Gothic church. So is the kind of decoration for the altar: the altar underneath is rich and elaborate and it was purposely hidden by beautiful coverings because people thought you should cover what was beautiful with something more beautiful still. And this screen here is later, about 1714, 1720, by the Derby smith Robert Bakewell, isn't it, who also did the vanes on the four pinnacles outside the church, and who did, I believe, the screen in Derby Cathedral.

Well, Archbishop Laud made a slight alteration to the arrangements of churches from what had been done in Queen Elizabeth's reign. The Puritans, the extreme people, or even the more conservative people, wanted one thing above everything, and that was – after this inaudibility and mystery – they wanted audibility and a congregation joining in and so they made churches into compartments. You had Matins and Evensong – those were the daily offices of the monks, the two services – in the church itself. Christening was done in another part of the church and sometimes there were pews differently arranged around the font and that was the baptistry. And Holy Communion was held in the chancel. And when the congregation said that prayer 'Draw near with faith', the people who were going to communicate came through the gates of the chancel, which were opened, and a guard stood at the gates to see that only those who were entitled to could come in, and the rest of the service went on behind the screen. And if you go to Foremark church, not far from here, always locked (the key is obtainable at the farm just beyond the church; they're quite pleased to let you have it. I can't think why it's locked) – if you go to Foremark church you will see there a survival of that Elizabethan worship although the fittings are 1662 – later than where we are here because there, in Foremark, there is a wooden screen through which it's very hard to see to the altar across the chancel arch, and all round the chancel walls are low seats for people to sit when they came through to the service at that part 'Draw near with faith'; and the altar, which is now against the east wall, was obviously originally in the middle of the chancel and the people sat round it and the priest stood at one end. That's the origin of the northward position that the evangelicals sometimes adopt though as a matter of fact, in origin, of course, it is high church.

The pews in Foremark church don't go along the back wall. What's quite different about this, and what was its innovation or rather return to the medieval, was that Archbishop Laud had the east wall made the sacred part of the church and the altar against the east wall as it is here, the sanctuary, very holy, and the crossing from the nave where you're sitting into the chancel comparatively simple and easy and open, so that the chancel, altar, nave, pulpit and font are all in one building and all connected and not so much cut off as they had been in the past. That was, I suppose, an oversimplification, but it's something to do with what the difference of Laudian worship is from others.

In this church, since we're on the subject, and just before I get to my final perorations (how long have I gone on for? oh, longer than I thought!) the east window is mid-Victorian. The windows in the chancel here, which you can't see but which I can, are late Georgian – I should think about 1820. The hatchments, which are perfectly beautiful and a great adornment to this kind of church, are eighteenth century. Now, there was a great deal of colour in seventeenth-century Church of England architecture. A lot of people think there wasn't at all, that everything was grey, that medieval people had everything brilliantly red and gold and then along came these dreary Anglicans who swept everything away. They didn't. It was full of colour and this church is still full of colour and you can still trace the Laudian idea of colour here in it. Up in the clerestory there are the old glass windows. Imagine this stained glass in the nave out and it all being clearish glass through which you can vaguely see the path and the cedars outside.

Then this screen, which I think has got a little too much gold on it, and the reds and blues of the 'achievements' as they were called – that is to say, the escutcheons or hatchments – and the ceiling, would look brighter still. So, when it was newer, would that velvet look more lovely; and that velvet, and those cushions there. But it was a very subtle delicate sense of colour they had, and it was quite different from a nineteenth-century sense of colour. Obviously when Burne-Jones was in favour and everything had to be green and natural, I can see why in the last century they didn't like the plaster that had been on the walls and took it off, and why they put in stained glass windows of that colour. *This* stained glass window is mid-Victorian; *these* are late Victorian. It was another sense of colour – and we are now coming back to the Laudian sense of colour, and

I think that the putting back of the plaster here has greatly restored it, and it certainly shows up the density of the colours of the ceilings, and it shows you that this church was all conceived by one man. Who he was I don't know but he was a mastermind. He had a perfectly clear idea. He was going to build a medieval church and he was going to add to it Renaissance fittings to fit in with the prayer book and he was going to have colour and light – and here, thank goodness, the colour and the light and the life are back.

There was one very beautiful little description that I was going to end with, though most of you will know it, and that is the bit – oh, by the way, there are some verses I must read you, they are frightfully good, about a country church in Georgian times. These are by Jane Taylor, who wrote 'Twinkle, Twinkle Little Star'. It's an absolutely unknown poem, it was first published in 1836 and it describes the squire's pew, and it's so lovely, here on this sunny Saturday afternoon, you could see it all again now:

> A slanting ray of evening light,
> Shoots through the yellow pane;
> It makes the faded crimson bright,
> And gilds the fringe again.
> The window's Gothic framework falls
> In oblique shadow on the walls.

The City churches

The Spectator, 5 November 1954

In the London Museum, when it was at Lancaster House, there used to be a delightful dark tunnel of models of old London, including one of the Great Fire itself. These models have lost their intimacy and character in the arid apple-green quarters of the new London Museum which is in the duller rooms of Kensington Palace. But it is still possible, by kneeling at the models so that the houses are at eye level, to imagine oneself back in the medieval City, where every house seemed to look like a cross between Staple Inn and Lavenham and where there were 108 City churches.

With this picture of a walled city, with red roofs and white stone and many turrets and a wide, slow-flowing Thames, held up from the sea by the sluice of waters under London Bridge, leave Kensington and go to Aldersgate Street. By going under the arch of the Star Inn in that street and turning left among the parked motors, you can still come out into the country. Silence reigns, and bracken and willow-herb and a few saplings grow among grass which covers a multitude of basements. A footpath toward the Middlesex-looking tower of St Giles', Cripplegate, leads in this country quiet to some large remains of the City wall. And as you see this great wall stretching ruinously towards Moorgate you can imagine yourself once more in the fields outside the ancient City. Though there are eight City churches which have survived, or at any rate partly survived both the Great Fire and the German bombs, only two of them, I think, bring back medieval London – St Bartholomew the Great and St Ethelburga's, Bishopsgate. The venerable and blackened Norman interior of St Bartholomew's is not improved by cement vaulting in the aisles and by the plethora of chairs, postcard tables, vases, brooms, ladders and other semi-sacred impedimenta of our dear old Church of England, and I really catch more of an idea of what the old churches of London before the Fire may have looked like from the humble little church of St Ethelburga.

Wren rebuilt 50 churches after the fire. Before the Germans came we had ourselves destroyed 19 of these. The Germans completely gutted 17 more Wren churches and there are now only 14 with their roofs on, and of these 3 are still shut to the public, which leaves us with 11 Wren churches open to us in the City, and precious indeed they are. Under the Archdeacon of London's far-sighted plan for the City churches, many more will be opened later when they are repaired or rebuilt.

Of those which survive for seeing today, I commend St Benet's, Paul's Wharf, which is Welsh and inclined to be locked, St Mary-at-Hill, St Magnus the Martyr, St Margaret's, Lothbury, St Margaret Pattens, St Peter's, Cornhill, and St Stephen's, Walbrook, as being the most characteristic Wren churches, comparatively unmolested by Victorian 'restoration'. St Mary-at-Hill, which is nothing to look at outside and surrounded by a smell of fish at Billingsgate, has the most untouched interior of all. Here the box pews, ironwork sword-rests, great west gallery, with its rich organ case, the fine pulpit and sounding board, the carved altar and altar-piece, recall Georgian London when beadles would hit the charity children sitting in the gallery with their staves, when merchants lived over their shops and offices, and pageboys carried the prayer books of rich widows before them as they walked to worship.

There were more such unrestored churches in the City nearly 40 years ago when I first knew it, for as a young boy I delighted to visit City churches, especially on a Sunday evening when single bells beat from moonlit steeples down gas-lit alleys, and choirboys would rush round corners through vestry archways. I can remember the row of fish-tail gaslights all along the triforium of St Bartholomew the Great; St Magnus the Martyr when it had box pews and seemed very dead, unlike the live and coloured place it is today; and St Alban's, Wood Street, with its green gas mantles and sparse congregation. In those days too, aged City men would come down from their brick, Italianate houses in Highbury or Streatham to worship in the City church where their fathers had worshipped before them. It was always my hope on some dark night to find a church which had escaped all the guide books and was there still in its classic splendour, with candles reflected in polished oak and cedar, with a parson in a black gown and bands, a beadle and the court of a City Company, robed and carrying a mace and swords. Once I thought I really had found the destroyed Wren church of St Matthew, Friday Street.

Where is the oratory of Prebendary Hine-Haycock, preaching to the ranks of Blue Coat boys, tier upon tier in the galleries of Christ Church, Newgate Street? Where is the dome of St Mildred's, Bread Street, under which I sat in a high pew to hear the words of the Revd Mr Richardson-Eyre, who would come in from some comfortable suburb to preach at Evensong on Sunday evening? Where is St Stephen's, Coleman Street, the plainest and most despised of Wren's churches? Where the evangelical raptures I enjoyed in St Bride's? Gone, gone, dead and bombed, only their peaceful memory now part of the history of our beautiful City.

Yet the bombing has done one service to Wren which makes up for the destruction which tall buildings and the commercial policy of the Church have done to his forest of steeples gathered round St Paul's. If you stand at the corner of Wood Street near the back of Goldsmiths Hall, in morning light or at night when the moon is up and there is a faint red glow in the sky from the West End, you will see what must be one of the most beautiful architectural sights in England. In the foreground withered willow-herb almost buries a pile of huge pink stones. Beyond this is Wren's exquisite stone steeple of St Vedast's, Foster Lane, less elaborate but more satisfying than his famous steeple of St Mary-le-Bow, which stands quite near. Beyond St Vedast's you will see the mighty dome of St Paul's and to the right the delicate and complicated silhouette of the northwest bell tower. And as you walk down Wood Street to Cheapside, St Vedast's steeple will glide past them and the hollows it will open to show the sky beyond. Here architecture does what all the best architecture should do. It moves as you go past it and changes to make another and another and another perfect picture.

I have left to the last those City churches built since the time of Wren and which architecturally are some of the best and, though I dare to say it, more impressive and inventive as interiors than those by Wren himself. I think the first indignation at vandalism I ever felt was over the destruction of the eighteenth-century brick church of St Catherine Coleman, Fenchurch Street, which happened between the wars. In those days people could swallow Wren but nothing later. Georgian was thought little of and St Catherine's was a complete untouched Georgian interior, with all its old woodwork. Since then, thank goodness, our appreciation has widened. But the Church has destroyed 8 of the 17 post-Wren churches in the City of London. Mercifully the Germans did little damage to 3 of the best, St Mary Woolnoth, All Hallows', London Wall, and St Botolph's, Aldersgate. Hawksmoor's church of St Mary Woolnoth by the Bank, with its twin square towers, is surely one of the most brilliant solutions to an awkwardly shaped site one could hope to see. The windowless side walls are full of interest. The interior with its top lights, though it is in fact small, seems majestic and enormous.

What is it that makes the City so different from all the rest of London? Mostly I think the City is different because of its churches, and these are used today more than ever, not just for concerts but as places in which to pray. If you go into the newly opened church of St James's, Piccadilly, you will find plenty of people about, but they are most of them standing and admiring the ornament. If you go into a City church you will generally find someone on his knees.

St Paul's the indestructible

Daily Telegraph, 23 May 1957

On certain Tuesday evenings in the month, when all the office workers have gone home and before the meat and fish markets have started their midnight thunder, the 12 bells of St Paul's are most beautifully rung for practice. Their notes, deep as an organ, pour over the empty offices and the towers and steeples of lesser churches and remind one that the City is the real old London, with its medieval lanes and courts, its ancient Guilds and little parishes.

The sound of the bells brings back old St Paul's before it was destroyed in the fire of 1666. It was the longest cathedral in England and in all Europe only St Peter's, Milan and Seville surpassed it in size. The golden eagle over its central spire dominated the flat Thames valley for miles, and the huge Gothic church rose high over the close-packed, clustering houses. The cathedral was the social centre of the city. Here, in the early morning, Mass was said daily at more than 30 lighted altars for the souls of the departed, while at the high altar the Mass of the people was celebrated. Behind high screens in the choir the offices of the Church were said throughout the day. The great nave of the church, the people's part, was full of hubbub so that the priests in the choir could hardly hear themselves say their offices. The nave was law courts, exchange, hiring-place and general meeting place of the City, infested with beggars and thieves as well as the respectable. Outside, at a stone octagon called Paul's Cross, sermons were preached on current abuses. Here Latimer inveighed against mercantile morals, here popery was denounced.

After reading a new history of St Paul's, edited by Dr W. R. Matthews, Dean of St Paul's, and the Revd W. M. Atkins, the cathedral's Librarian, I realize that neither preaching heresy at St Paul's Cross, nor causing scandal and brawling in Paul's nave, nor the Reformation, plagues, fires, nor even Cromwell, have destroyed the tradition of this, the only cathedral in England to be known by the name of its Saint rather than that of the city in which it stands. The encouragement of Charles II, the genius of Wren, his protégé, and the affection and generosity of the citizens of London raised the St Paul's we see today. What I had forgotten was the long sequence of ecclesiastics from AD 604 until today who have kept the cathedral alive, even though at times in the past four centuries it may have seemed to be nearly dead.

St Paul's was not a monastic foundation, and because of this the dean can be outvoted by the four other canons in his chapter. 'Dr Inge once wrote that he felt like a mouse surrounded by four cats, meaning, one fears, the residentiary canons. It is tempting to add, in Churchillian language, "Some mouse!"' Deans and chapters are not always on good terms with their bishops. Nor are deans and canons always on good terms with one another. This history of them makes entertaining reading, and despite quarrellers, place men, pluralists and heretics there has always been someone with a genuine desire to improve the lot of the poor and teach the ignorant the catechism.

The story includes great names – deans such as Colet, John Donne, Milman, Gregory, Church and Inge; archbishops like Bancroft, Laud and Tillotson; canons such as Sydney Smith, Liddon, Scott Holland and Alexander and minor canons like R. H. Barham, author of the *Ingoldsby Legends*. There are plenty of entertaining incidents. For instance, the amiable churchman Joseph Butler, a Georgian dean and bishop of Bristol in plurality, said to John Wesley: 'Sir, the pretending to extraordinary revelation and gifts of the Holy Spirit is a horrid thing, a very horrid thing.' Mendelssohn one Sunday afternoon in 1829 played the cathedral organ for so long that the vergers, impatient to go home, persuaded the blowers to let the wind out of the instrument. Sydney Smith, complaining of the cold in the cathedral in the winter, said: 'My sentences are frozen as they come out of my mouth and thawed in the course of the summer, making strange noises and unexpected assertions in different parts of the church.'

The successors of these wits and saints and strong personalities live today in two rows of houses at Amen Court within a stone's throw of the cathedral. You may see them in their plane-shaded quiet if you trespass on their private road. There they are, the canons and minor canons writing their sermons among their books. London is a cathedral city and this is its Barchester with the dean across the road.

The last great days of St Paul's were in Victorian times, when Liddon's wonderful preaching crowded the cathedral to capacity. But in those times a great mistake was made in the interior. The screen and organ above it, which shut off the choir from the dome and nave, were taken away. What had been a vista with mystery and a suggestion of greater riches beyond the screen became a long tunnel. Today a visitor sitting at the back of the nave could not see what is going on at the altar without a telescope, and it is very hard to pray with a telescope. Moreover, the proportions of Wren's choir were destroyed by the removal of the screen, and the new baldacchino will not improve them.

Outside, the cathedral is unsurpassed. I do not think Wren meant the design to be seen all at once. He meant you to get glimpses down lanes and turnings. Stand in Ivy Lane, off Newgate Street, and you will see St Paul's as Wren intended. In the foreground is his restored chapter house, coming up to the height of the bottom row of columns along the body of the building. The Victorians exceeded that height all round the cathedral. Our own age built Faraday House, which is the worst insult yet to St Paul's, worse even than the railway bridge at the foot of Ludgate Hill, lately made uglier by having its latticed parapet boxed in with solid panelling.

Whenever I look up from Fleet Street at the dome of Paul's and its shadowy Portland stone, bell towers and portico crowning Ludgate Hill, I am uplifted by the beauty of Wren's architecture. His 'model' design in the shape of a cross was rejected by the dean and chapter because they wanted a cathedral on the medieval plan with a long choir shut off from the dome and nave by a screen. Wren gave it them. St Paul's seems to me symbolic of our Church. It is a medieval plan on an ancient foundation rebuilt in the Renaissance style of its time. It is both catholic and reformed.

Wolfhampcote church

The Spectator, 3 January 1958

I must recount a curious incident about the church at Wolfhampcote, near Daventry, for the removal of which to a building estate in Coventry proposals are now being made. It is a mottled stone building of medieval date, consisting of tower, nave, aisles and chancel, and standing alone in a field below a railway embankment and approached by gated, unmetalled roads. My friend John Piper and I visited it one autumn evening shortly after the war. It was locked and deserted and the sunset colours were scooped into the curves of the crown-glass Georgian windows, where they were unshattered. We discovered the key in a distant cottage, but it would not turn in the lock, and we eventually climbed in through one of the broken windows. It was a perfect un-'restored' village church, with traces of painting on the walls, fading monuments, old woodwork. The altar frontal was lifted up, revealing a black hole beyond it. In the failing light we could see steps going down from this hole to rows of coffins in the passage of a mausoleum attached to the east end of the church, and externally in the Strawberry Hill Gothick style. It was the vault of the Tibbets family, whose crest is a cat.

As it was now dark, John Piper visited the church to make drawings on another day with someone else. While they were there, a little man, neatly dressed and carrying a bag, arrived and walked into the church by the locked door without any difficulty. After a time they went in to see what he was doing, and found that he had rifled a chest in the church and had put on some vestments and was swinging incense about. He had lit candles on the altar. They asked him what he was doing and he said he often came there and thought a little incense did the church good. He seemed anxious for them to go away, and indeed he outstayed them. Was he a madman or was he intending to say a Black Mass above the vault of the Tibbets? The question remains unanswered, but the atmosphere in the church was certainly creepy, and if this lovely but mysterious building is to be moved I hope it will be speeded on its way with a service of reconciliation, which will have to be performed by the bishop, as this is a consecrated building.

Gordon Square church

from *The University Church of Christ the King: A Brief History* (1964)

I am so glad that you are being allowed to use the Catholic Apostolic church in Gordon Square as a chapel for London University. Good heavens! You couldn't have a grander chapel. Why, even the nave of Westminster Abbey is only 13 feet higher than the nave and sanctuary of Gordon Square. You have not got just a chapel for London University, but a cathedral.

What I wanted to tell you was how splendid I think it as a building. As you know there was to be a spire 150 feet high over the tower crossing, and the nave was to extend two bays further west. This last would perfect the proportions of what is, without a doubt, the grandest church in London of the pioneer days of the Gothic Revival. We may be ahead of our time in seeing its beauty now (though its beauty ought to be obvious to anyone who isn't a silly prig mesmerized by dates and prejudiced against Victorian because he's afraid of being thought old-fashioned), but I'm quite sure that in ten years' time you will be thankful for having so magnificent and uplifting a building for worship.

It isn't until you are inside that you get its full grandeur. Its architect, J. Raphael Brandon, wrote what is the standard work on *Open Timber Roofs*, and another on *Parish Churches* (with his brother who died in 1847, aged 26), and the famous *Analysis of Gothic Architecture*. The Gordon Square church was started at a time (1833) when people were beginning to learn about medieval architecture thoroughly and systematically. As with the Roman and Greek orders – the last well displayed in Wilkins' design for London University in Gower Street – it was considered wrong to depart from precedent. You will therefore find in the Gordon Square church that Brandon did much careful copying of details from great abbeys (the corbels at the tower crossing, by the way, were done by someone else in 1895, and very lively and rich they are), just as Wilkins copied from Greek details for his university building. But you will find in Gordon Square the something extra which raises it out of mere copying into grand architecture – an overall sense of proportion. Stand at the extreme west end and look east. Notice how the hammer-beam roof with its rich carving soars almost out of sight, becomes a stone-vaulted roof over the sanctuary, and then leads the eye down the long-drawn vista to the pinnacled tabernacle, the personal gift of Brandon to the church, on the high altar. Beyond it, open tracery hints at the richest part of all the church, the apostles' chapel with its painted timber roof and deeply cut stone sedilia.

The broad sanctuary will give you a wide space for congregational and eucharistic worship in which all can join. For daily and smaller services there is the apostles' chapel, and room for side chapels. Everywhere vistas, everywhere dignity, and above all mystery – Gordon Square church is solemn and suited to the mystery of religion. It is built for worship not for lectures. There is nothing shoddy or ill-made anywhere. All had to be of the best for the glory of God, and the Catholic Apostolic Church members give a tithe of their income to the church. Change as few details as you can, especially leave altar fittings and lights. The seven lamps, for instance, are a sort of veil between the altar and the nave (the sanctuary lamp beyond them was designed by Pugin for Drummond), and the brass and carved wood and grisaille glass in the windows are all part of the time it was built, still serve their purposes admirably, and are increasingly appreciated year by year. The church was built for the noble ritual of the Catholic Apostolic Church which was a mixture of our own, the Roman Catholic, and the Orthodox liturgies. I remember the 'Angel' (Bishop) sitting in his canopied throne by the altar when the church was lit by gas and better attended than it came to be. Do have a look at the Catholic Apostolic liturgy if you haven't done so already. I am always sad that the second coming which the Catholic Apostolic Church so ardently expects has been so delayed that all the apostles who founded the church in 1835 are dead (the last died in 1901) and now all the angels are dead. The church still has adherents here and in North Germany and America, and it certainly had plenty of money – including that of the Drummonds and the Percys – for building splendid churches of which your chapel to be and the Pearson church on the canal in Maida Vale are the two best of the seven in London. I hope you will live to see the two bays added to the nave of Gordon Square church.

Westminster Abbey

Prologue to *Westminster Abbey*, ed. A. L. Rowse (1972)

Westminster Abbey is different things to different people.

To the *dévoué* it is the shrine containing the bones of its founder, St Edward the Confessor. Annual pilgrimages are made to it not only by members of the Church of England but by Roman Catholics, whose Cathedral is Bentley's magnificent basilica further down the road towards Victoria Station. For all the English it is the place where every monarch since William the Conqueror (except for Edward V and Edward VIII) has been consecrated with oil and crowned. For antiquaries it is Thorney Island. There are stone vestiges of St Edward the Confessor's original Saxon abbey. For architects the present church and its great octagonal chapter house are an exemplar of the Gothic style. Here in nave, transept and cloister is the tall French architecture of the reign of Henry III when England was an integral part of Christendom. It is purest Early English, started in 1376 and continuing to be used in the building of the nave until 1528, a remarkable survival of a strong plain style triumphing over fashion. At the east end is the last exuberant Tudor outburst of Gothic in Henry VII's Chapel, fan-vaulted English Perpendicular within, sheltering elaborate early Renaissance coloured monuments and gilded ironwork. Outside from across the Thames, Henry VII's Chapel must have looked like an elaborate galleon, for its pinnacles were topped with little gold pennons and vanes.

To the boys of Westminster School 'up Abbey' means going to the abbey for their school chapel. In it they have daily services. The monks who served St Peter's Abbey, which the Confessor founded, were Benedictines and a teaching order. Boys were first taught by the monks, it is said, in the western cloister. There was also a grammar school west of the abbey in the precincts. Queen Elizabeth I refounded the two schools as a single institution which is the present Westminster School. The dean is *ex officio* chairman of its governors. In the abbey at coronations its scholars have the right to acclaim the monarch first. In the eighteenth century it was the greatest public school in England, and it is still one of them. For those interested in monumental sculpture the abbey is unrivalled in the kingdom.

It has the handsomest tombs of every age from the medieval to the present. To the liturgiologist the services of the abbey and its customs make it a unique survival. The late minor canon and sacrist, Jocelyn Perkins, wrote three volumes for the Alcuin Club on Westminster Abbey, its worship and ornaments (1938–52). The dean, canons, minor canons, and sacrist in their enviable houses about the precincts are the successors of the Benedictine monks. The surveyor, organist, vergers, masons and those concerned with the fabric are the equivalent of the lay-brothers of the medieval community.

For historians it is the burial place of our kings, queens, courtiers, statesmen, lawyers, writers, generals and particularly admirals and naval officers. Though one could not say that the poets buried in Poets' Corner run the whole gamut of Palgrave's *Golden Treasury*, they are a memorable group.

Joseph Addison in a paper to *The Spectator* for Friday, 30 March 1711 said:

> Upon going into the Church, I entertained myself with the digging of a Grave; and saw in every Shovel-full of it that was thrown up, the Fragment of a Bone or Skull intermixt with a kind of fresh moulder-ing Earth that some time or other had a place in the Composition of an human Body. Upon this, I began to consider with myself what innumerable Multitudes of People lay confused together under the Pavement of that ancient Cathedral; how Men and Women, Friends and Enemies, Priests and Soldiers, Monks and Prebendaries, were crumbled amongst one another, and blended together in the same common Mass; how Beauty, Strength, and Youth, with Old-age, Weak-ness, and Deformity, lay undistinguished in the same promiscuous Heap of Matter.

Or there was Max Beerbohm's essay on the abbey's wax effigies, 'The Ragged Regiment', from *Yet Again* (1909).

Certainly, such of us as reside in London take Westminster Abbey as a matter of course. A few of us will be buried in it, but meanwhile we don't go to it, even as we don't go to the Tower, or the Mint, or the Monument. Only for some special purpose do we go – as to hear a sensational bishop preaching, or to see a monarch anointed. And on these rare occasions we cast but a casual glance at the abbey – that close-packed chaos of beautiful things and worthless vulgar things. That the abbey should be thus chaotic does not seem strange to us; for lack of orderliness and discrimination is an essential characteristic of English genius. But to the Frenchman, with his passion for symmetry and harmony, how very strange it must all seem!

I suppose I was five when I first saw it. At that age there was the impression that it was only the south transept. For most visitors, until recently, this was the chief entrance open to the public. One glanced in, the crowds were great, the place was tall and dark and surprisingly short for something so tall. I did not walk as far as the tower-crossing nor did I look down the nave nor up to those three exquisite arches behind the high altar. It was not until I was nine or ten that I was taken to the royal tombs and Henry VII's Chapel. These did not seem as interesting to me then as the Tower of London and Traitor's Gate. There were not enough ghosts. In those days I did not know that the bodies of Cromwell's government had been disinterred at the Restoration and thrown into a deep pit outside the abbey and their decapitated heads displayed over Westminster Hall. I thought that anything really old and to be revered had to be round-arched and Norman. As for the kings and tombs and effigies, they were a spate of words of vergers or schoolmasters or guides and too many to be taken in.

At the age of 16 or 17 one reacts against the opinions of one's parents. Mine admired the Gothic and the abbey particularly, because it was Gothic and historic, two qualities of perfection. I was already tending towards the Georgian and had begun to admire the Baroque sculpture of Roubiliac and the pioneer investigation by Mrs Esdaile of eighteenth-century monuments. Partly to annoy my parents and old-fashioned schoolmasters, and also partly within myself, I then preferred St Paul's. When I came to work in London, after the usual two-year period of teaching in preparatory schools, my friend John Edward Bowle, the historian, had been made sixth-form history master at Westminster School. Thus I was able to discover the armoury and the little cloister with its splashing fountain and its unforgettable view of Barry's Victoria Tower. I also discovered the main cloisters. As to the canons and clergy, I knew none of them; they seemed to me semi-royal. The precincts of the abbey, though they are blessedly open during most of the day, still have a forbiddingly private look.

As a journalist on the *Architectural Review* in Queen Anne's Gate, I found the abbey a dominating presence. Those two western towers completed by Nicholas Hawksmoor, in his own version of Gothic, were to be seen every day down Tothill Street. A reproach to them, we modernists must have felt, was Charles Holden's London Transport building, built in 1929, with its plain square tower in the latest modern unadorned functional style, and carved insets by Henry Moore, Eric Gill and others. This seemed the true Gothic. All the same there was the deeper call of the truer Gothic, when all ten bells rolled out on state occasions and when the lesser smaller melodious ring could be heard after fashionable weddings in St Margaret's.

In those days the interior of the abbey was dark and dingy. The great Lethaby seemed to have concentrated on keeping the structure standing, and I have been told that his only artistic contribution was the rather inadequate brass electroliers. There were many things for a forward-looking architectural journalist to criticize. For instance the lettering on the unknown warrior's grave seemed a very long way from Eric Gill. It still seems so, and must have come from a monumental mason and been ordered by the foot and acquiesced in by the dean and chapter, who were only interested in the wording. But now I do not know that art is all that important in an inspired idea like this. In a way, this famous slab typifies the abbey and that touch of the commonplace and the numinous which make it different from anywhere else.

Since the war the abbey has been transformed inside and has flowered. The new surveyor, Stephen Dykes Bower (appointed in 1951), first cleaned the stone, and we realized that the grey Purbeck of the Henry III columns was designed to contrast with the cream-coloured Caen stone. The paintings on the vaulted roof became visible, including arabesques designed by Wren around the bosses. The early Renaissance monuments were startlingly restored to their full colour, which brought back the swagger and delightful vulgarity of the New Learning. The monument to Henry Carey, 1st Baron Hunsdon, in St John the Baptist's Chapel off the north ambulatory, must be the biggest in any church in England. The cleaning of the walls showed up the splendour of the eighteenth-century glass, particularly that in the west window. The noble, white marble statues of Georgian and Victorian days were cleaned.

The internal glory has been almost wholly restored, yet the heart of the abbey, the shrine of its founder, is a caricature of a shrine. It was despoiled in 1540, and though the relics are still inside it, the mosaics have been picked out from the stonework and its columns damaged. All this could easily be restored to what it was like when Henry III rebuilt the shrine. The Cosmati work with which it was adorned could be put back by modern craftsmen.

One of the first of the Victorian restorers of the abbey was Edward Blore, who designed the choir screen in 1834. Greatly daring, the present surveyor applied full colour to this screen and to the stalls within the choir, which had later been restored by Sir Gilbert Scott, whose masterpiece is the restored chapter house. This lightening of the former dinginess of the abbey shows up how good Victorian work can be. Its proportions and detail are emphasized by bright-coloured paint and they are well suited to their surroundings, as is the restored stained glass in the chapter house. Let us hope that this book will bring about the completion of the interior restoration of the abbey. For the floors of nave and transepts, at present of inferior Portland stone, should be of more durable material, such as marble, to withstand the onslaught of thousands of shoes.

The chief delight of Westminster Abbey for the Londoner can be its daily services. I remember with embarrassment some satirical verses I wrote before the war on official religion connected with the abbey. After the war, when I deteriorated into becoming a committee man, I sat on a commission whose offices were close by. After these painful and often boring sessions, it was a relief to come out into the open air. More often than not the two bells were ringing for Evensong, then I would go in to the service and be ushered into a seat near the choir. The evening light would fade from the stained glass. Softened electric light threw mysterious shadows. The well-known prayer-book phrases were read by priests in canopied stalls. An anthem by Lawes or Weelkes or some unrecognized Victorian musician soared to the vaulting. The commission and the arguments fell into proportion and ceased to irritate. The traffic roar in Parliament Square, the 11s and the 24s, were muffled by the buttressed building. Even more than state occasions and memorial services, these weekday Evensongs have impressed me. The abbey is more of an ancient abbey still at an 8 a.m. communion service in one of the side chapels, with only a few there.

For the purpose of writing this introduction, I was taken on a final tour of the place by the archdeacon, Canon Carpenter. It was a summer evening after the church had been shut. I walked to his house just as the gas-lights were being turned on in the cloisters and cobbled passages of the royal surroundings of the abbey. I was in the London of Dickens. As we passed the chapter house, I remarked on how strange it was that this building, so well restored by Sir Gilbert Scott, was in the care of the Department of the Environment, and not of the dean and chapter. He pointed out that it had been the scene of the first English Parliament in the royal palace of Westminster and that it represented what the abbey stands for, the tension between the present and the past. As we came into the nave by the south-west door, someone was playing the organ. There was a lay brother (i.e. a verger) on duty. The stained glass in the west window, gold, blue, dark red and silver, was at its Georgian armorial grandest. I saw the point of those crystal chandeliers, which were presented to the abbey by the

Guinness family after the last war. The lay brother turned them on and they gradually swelled in brightness, though there was never a glare. We walked round the tombs, up to St Edward's shrine, over the engineer's new bridge leading to it. This is as inoffensive as it is practical. We went into Henry VII's Chapel, and had a look at the praying hands of Margaret Beaufort. The lights were turned down into semi-darkness as we came out into the gas-lit mystery of the cloister and past the hall of Westminster School close by the deanery – that hall inside looks like a Georgian aquatint of the hall of a Cambridge college.

As I write these final sentences in a City of London precinct near the Norman church of Rahere's Priory of St Bartholomew the Great, the Corporation of London dust-cart is making a hellish noise under my window. There is always a tension between the past and the present. In Westminster Abbey the tension for most of us is created by the thousands of tourists of all nations and faiths who queue, apparently without comprehension, through a place which means much to us. But do they not understand? I think they do. Their shuffling presence remains after the doors are shut. Finally, at the south end of the south transept hidden away, is the chapel of St Faith. This is for me the part of the abbey where tension between past and present ceases.

The Grosvenor Chapel

Introduction to *Godly Mayfair*, ed. Ann Callender (1980)

I have always liked things which hide themselves. This the Grosvenor Chapel certainly does. From the outside you would never know what a surprise awaited you architecturally. Outside it is a little piece of New England in warm old London brick set down amid fashionable Dutch revival commercial premises of the eighties onwards.

It is the chapel's quietness and obscurity which have made me fond of it, and the fact that it is high church, which I was brought up and am. I first went there because it was a continuation of the Oxford I had known and loved as an undergraduate in the twenties, and I have always liked its associations with Oxford. It was run in those days by Philip Usher, an unassuming, quiet and scholarly priest like Wilfred Derry who later followed him. I went because of Freddie Hood. He was such a good man. You could see when he looked out at you through his wire spectacles that he knew everything about you: his eyes twinkled with understanding and affection.

On the whole, what makes Grosvenor Chapel perfect for me is that people never bother you there. The whole point of it is that you aren't asked to join something. The joy of going there is that you aren't being welcomed into a club and made to go to parties and take part in things. You are left alone, but at the same time you aren't cold-shouldered.

I remember getting to know the chapel better in Father Whiteman's day, because Rose Macaulay was a good friend of mine, and she loved Father Whiteman. Once, when the ice was very cold and thick on the Serpentine, it was said Rose petitioned Father Whiteman to break it so that she could bathe. When dear old Joad was dying of cancer, Father Whiteman used to bring the sacrament out from Grosvenor Chapel to Hampstead, and Rose and I used to attend mass there in his house with Father Whiteman as the celebrant.

Another reason why I belong to Grosvenor Chapel is that its depth and beauty have grown on me. I do not think that it is even necessary to complete Comper's uncompleted scheme. The building has got a little bit of mystery to it in its unfinished state. Comper had an absolutely unerring sense of where to put things. Grosvenor Chapel is a real church with mystery in it. It is a real adornment to Mayfair. It is in the natural material of London, which is brick. It partakes of the Thames Valley, although its interior is by an Aberdonian Scot. And it has got a surprising greatness of scale, which you would not guess from the outside. It is also extremely comfortable: it is upholstered religion for the rich.

The preaching tradition is fine. The best preacher I know is John Gaskell. I am very glad to say that I am a sermon taster, and I have never heard better sermons than his. He has the natural melody of language in his words. He is obviously a poet. In fact, Grosvenor Chapel is a most surprising church in that it is such a poetical place. We don't want argument. We want to be carried away into the heavens, as we are there. And when we step out and we see Purdey's, it's very surprising – everything is a surprising contrast.

Part 4

THE CHRISTIAN LIFE

'It's never easy, the Christian life, and the more effort it demands, the more worth keeping up it is.'

Letter to Oliver Stonor, 7 August 1948

St Petroc

BBC Radio, 11 July 1949

St Petroc died in Cornwall more than 1,200 years ago. The sixth and seventh centuries in which he lived are a sort of Bodmin Moor, an unknown territory. Worse than that, they are a no man's land between the archaeologists and the historians of early Christian Britain. Archaeologists, who are generally ardent unbelievers, dismiss the period as 'Late Iron Age'. Writers of our church history take an almost unchristian pleasure in contradicting one another's statements about those remote centuries. The late Revd S. Baring-Gould, the most readable and enjoyable writer on the Celtic Church, is, alas!, regarded as unreliable. To him I owe all my early enthusiasm. The late Canon Doble, a scholar who did more than any man to find out about the Cornish saints, wrote mainly for scholars. If it were not for his pamphlet about St Petroc (third edition 1938) we would know hardly anything of St Petroc at all. What I say tonight is little more than a condensing and rearranging of some of the finds Canon Doble made. If a wireless talk can be dedicated to anyone's memory, this should be to that of Canon Doble, vicar of Wendron.

Strange and sweet-sounding saints of Cornwall – Morwenna, Monofroda, Endoliontra, Ladoc, Cadoc, Kow, Cuby and Tudy and all the rest of you! – come to my aid and help me to present, here on the wireless, a picture of the greatest of your number, Holy Petroc, Abbot and Confessor! Thirty or forty churches in the West bear Petroc's name: Padstow, Little Petherick, Bodmin and Trevalga in Cornwall, three churches in Wales, two in Somerset, twelve in Devon, many in Brittany. Here in his own kingdom, where he lived and died, St Petroc is rarely remembered. But in Brittany his cult survives: hymns are sung to him; he is a fisherman's saint and in one place his statue is taken out and whipped if the fishing is bad. One of his statues there shows him as a small, benevolent-looking, bearded man, in spotted vesture, holding a book in his left hand while with his right he pats a stag that has jumped up at him. In Brittany, too, the life of St Petroc has been preserved. Canon Doble translated it into English. In 1937 a British Museum official found another *Life of St Petroc* in the Ducal Library of Gotha in Germany. They were not all that different

125

from one another, and neither of them was authoritative, because they were written hundreds of years after St Petroc's death, but they contain local Cornish folklore about our beloved saint.

Put very shortly, this is something of what they said. Petroc was the son of a Welsh king. When his father died, he could have become king himself. He decided instead to be a monk and called together 60 followers and friends and asked them if they wanted to join him. They agreed to do so and sailed together to Ireland, where in those dark ages of Europe the light of learning and Christianity burned brightest. There they stayed in the monasteries of the Church. A monastery was a street of little stone cells in a walled enclosure containing also an oratory for praying and a church for worship. All the buildings were made of unmortared stones, like a drystone wall, and roofed with a dome of balanced stones. They were set beside streams or wells, even on the tops of great island rocks rising hundreds of feet from the ocean.

After 20 years of study in Ireland, Petroc and his followers sailed to Cornwall and landed in the Camel estuary, stepping ashore at Trebetherick – the place of Petroc. Here they found some men harvesting who were rude to them and laughed at their funny clothes. Petroc himself carried a staff and a small bell like a sheep bell. Many missionaries had been coming to the heathen Cornish at this time. 'We're thirsty, give us fresh water,' said the harvesters, by way of testing his sanctity. Petroc struck a rock and a spring appeared before their eyes. So then he asked them where the nearest religious man was – for Celtic tribal life was in two parts, religious and worldly, each with its own enclosures and rules of life and working arrangements with its neighbours. The harvesters pointed to the other side of the river, where a hermit named Samson lived at Lolissick. Near him lived a bishop called Wethnoc. Bishops were humble men then, less important than abbots of monasteries and used for confirming and consecrating rather than for administration. Wethnoc gave his cell to Petroc and thus the monastery was founded known to this day as Petrocstow, which we now pronounce Padstow. Here Petroc lived a strict life. When he felt evil desires on him, he stood in a cold stream. He ate bread only – except on Sundays, when he had porridge. On fast days he ate ashes with his bread. He and his monks ground their corn at Little Petherick mill and built an oratory beside it.

One day his companions were grumbling about the weather. 'It will be fine tomorrow,' said Petroc. But it was not. So Petroc accused himself of presumption in thinking he could prophesy about the weather and decided to go on a pilgrimage to Rome as a penance for his presumption. Then he went to Jerusalem, to the Lord's sepulchre, and the 'thirst, hunger, sweat and cold and night-watching which he had endured for the name of Christ on the way, he counted as delights'. Then, sleeping by the seashore of India, to which he had gone, he woke to see a boat full of light floating towards him. This he entered and was carried to an island where he lived for seven years on fish. Then he returned to Cornwall and found his sheepskin cloak and his staff on the seashore and a wolf guarding it which accompanied him until he came back to his companions at Padstow.

A local king called Tendor kept poisonous snakes and horrible reptiles and centipedes in a marshy lake. But when this lake was no longer used for punishing criminals, the hungry monsters started eating each other until only one was left – a hideous creature of enormous size, its body swelled with all the snakes and centipedes it had eaten. It ravaged the neighbourhood. But Petroc boldly went up to it, bound it with his holy stole and led it away. As he was leading it along, a huge funeral came in view, and the mourners were so astonished and terrified at the sight of this fearful monster, they fell on the ground. Petroc went to the coffin and brought the body of the young man who lay in it to life. He then released the monster and ordered it to hurt no more people, and it went away beyond the sea.

One day when Petroc was praying, a stag came running towards him pursued by hounds and huntsmen. Petroc protected the animal, and the huntsmen did not dare to touch it while it was being cared for by a religious man. Then Constantine, the chief of the huntsmen, appeared and raised his sword to slay Petroc, but he was struck with paralysis and could move neither hand nor foot. Then the saint prayed and Constantine was released, and he and all his men were converted to Christ.

A great dragon that lived near Petroc's cell on the moor got a piece of wood into its right eye. It ran to Petroc's church and laid its head on the entrance step for three days, waiting for a miracle. By Petroc's command it was sprinkled with water mingled with dust of the church floor, and straightaway the wood was removed and the dragon's sight restored, and it returned to its accustomed wallowing place.

After 60 years in and about Padstow and Little Petherick, after performing many more kindnesses and miracles, Petroc commended his monks to the care of him whom he had chosen as his successor. Taking one companion he journeyed to Bodmin, and there in a remote wooded valley he found a holy hermit living alone whose name was Vuron. Vuron offered Petroc his cell and himself moved one day's journey southward. There, between two mountains and by a streamside, Petroc lived and prayed, visited by his monks and his successor.

When he felt that he was dying, Petroc set out to Little Petherick and Padstow to say goodbye to his monks there. But on his way from Little Petherick at a place called Treravel, where the footpath leaves the road and crosses the fields to Padstow, Petroc felt he could go no further. The man of the house took him in and there on the night of the fourth of June he died, and his soul shone like a star in the room where his dead body lay. And they say that whoever was ill in the farmhouse of Treravel (the old building, not the present one) had to be taken out of the house before he could die.

St Petroc was buried at Padstow and his remains were taken to Bodmin in the tenth century when the Danes pillaged Padstow. There they were kept in the priory church until in 1177 an angry Bodmin monk stole them and took them to St Moen Abbey in Brittany. Henry II ordered the abbot of St Moen to return them to the prior of Bodmin. So they came back and at Winchester, Henry II and his court venerated St Petroc's relics and the monks returned with them to Bodmin, carrying them in a beautiful box that Henry II gave to them. This box survives in a Bodmin bank. It is 10 inches by 18, faced with white ivory and bound with brass, and on the ivory are engraved birds picked out in golden roundels. But St Petroc's bones are no longer there.

One last and thrilling discovery about St Petroc was made just lately by a monk of Downside Abbey. He has identified the beehive cell by the streamside of the empty farm of Fernacre on Bodmin Moor as the dwelling that St Vuron gave up to St Petroc. Whether it was the cell or not, I do not know. While historians and archaeologists fight it out, let us go in spirit, as last year I did in the flesh, to that lonely valley between Rough Tor and Brown Willy. Fernacre Farm is granite, its garden walls are granite and there, before short and deep-grown grass by a streamside, is St Petroc's cell.

It is made of granite boulders and stones, stuffed in between with grassy turf. Inside, one can stand upright in the middle, for the top of the dome is seven feet high. Sunset shone on the entrance of the cell – Rough Tor, sprinkled with sacred stones, on one side, Brown Willy's heathery slopes upon the other. Not a motor car, nor aeroplane, nor modern sound was heard, only sheep bleating and larks singing and the startled thud of a nearby moorland pony. A silence so deep and so long that the chirps and scurryings of nature only made it greater. Here, as to St Petroc, because nature was near, so was the Creator. Time disappeared. The Celtic Church tinkled in Cornwall with the bells of its saints expecting Christ at any moment. Here on Bodmin Moor it would be no shock to see the bearded form of Petroc, with stags, poultry and wolves following him, not bothering to eat one another, for devotion to the saint.

The persecution of country clergy

Time and Tide, 17 March 1951

Townspeople do not know of the persecution which the English country clergy endure, at any rate south of the Trent. And some villages may not be as uncharitable to their parsons as others. Most villages have one faithful family and perhaps two or three people of true humility, ready to put up with the parson. Yet I will be surprised if at least a few of the circumstances I am about to describe do not exist in every English village.

We hear much about how bad the worldly portion of country clergymen is, how vast their rectories, how inadequate their income to the social position expected of them. Their spiritual plight is often far worse. Let us imagine a parson, young or old, coming with perfectly definite views, catholic or evangelical, to an English village. Let him be a man with a real love of souls, courageously uncompromising about Truth and not prepared to water it down to suit the consciences of his flock on the off-chance of filling an empty pew.

Let us imagine a village of the usual modern structure. The large house a ruin or a government office, the late squire's unmarried daughter living in a cottage, two or three immensely prosperous farmers, a few weekenders, a few farm workers to drive tractors, a bus collecting most able-bodied people to a factory outside the nearest town, a bus collecting the men, women and children to the cinema once or twice a week in the evening. Other nights are occupied by dances and whist drives. The rulers of the village are the innkeeper at one end and the schoolteacher at the other. The farmers live their own lives among other farmers' families. Their women folk take only a sporadic interest in the Women's Institute, which is run by a schoolmistress or the squire's daughter (rarely by both) for the wives of the farm workers. The young men and the young girls think they are film stars and talk with American accents, go away on bicycles and buses every evening, or else play together in the social club.

The wireless is on in every cottage as the remover's van arrives at the parsonage. Curtains are drawn aside, invalids peep with malevolent eyes from leaded windows, gossips lean on gates, young men and old happen to be casually walking by. What will the new parson be like?

On that first Sunday his church, for the first and last time of his incumbency, will be nearly full. After the service, the village will be agreed on one point only – that his predecessor was much better. Some will think him too 'high', others too 'low'. What most of them will mean is that he is different from the man before. Villagers are notoriously ignorant of theology but conservative about ritual.

The people who may continue to go to church are the following. The late squire's daughter, because of church and state and her late father's views. But woe betide the parson if he tries to change anything or teach anything except vague morality. This will mean that no Labour people will go, that is to say no farm workers because going to church means you are Conservative. The bell-ringers may continue because of the pleasure of ringing and because they admire Winston Churchill. The schoolmistress will not go, even if it is a church school she is teaching in, because being semi-educated and class-conscious, she has 'theories' about religion and regards the parson as too dogmatic. She will attempt to disaffect the children and their mothers.

A young girl and her friend will go for a week or two because she has fallen in love with the new parson. The innkeeper will not go because if he is to please his employers, the brewers, he must not seem to take sides. The farmers will not go except at Harvest Festival because the collections are for the Farmers' Benevolent, the only charity they allow themselves to notice. Everyone feels there is no need to please any landlord any more. The village is independent, materialistic and, like all villages, a bit out of date compared with the towns where people are coming back to church.

Except the 'prog' weekenders, now rather elderly, who take in the *New Statesman*, all villagers will use the church, of course, for baptisms and burials – the Registry Office is becoming increasingly popular for village weddings. The parson may think this use of the church is a sign that his people are Christian at heart. More probably it is a sign that they are superstitious, in the way we are about walking under a ladder.

If he is prepared to have a breezy word for everyone, give liberally of his small stipend to all funds and do a great many secretarial and transport and listening jobs free, his fence will not be pulled down, the church may sometimes be cleaned (for a fee) and he and his family will be tolerated.

But if he teaches religion, if he attempts to be definite, if he admonishes and exhorts, if he really loves God and his neighbour fearlessly, he will be despised and rejected when not actually mocked. Scandals will be spread about him and the witch-like malice of the self-righteous will fall on him.

The pride of the semi-educated, the anger of the greedy farmer will flourish in village sloth. 'Many country people think there is something in all this religion,' as Samuel Gurney says, 'and they aren't going to have anything to do with it.' The country parson's cross is heavy with their apathy and sharp with their hate. He sees his failure round him every day. Only the very few help him to bear it. Small wonder if sometimes he falls.

The Victorian Sunday

BBC Radio, 10 July 1951

I went for a walk on the Berkshire Downs with Bishop Shedden, the vicar of Wantage. I am not a Victorian myself. He says he is. What I tell you now are largely his impressions.

I think the first thing we would have noticed would have been the quiet. No mireless on, neither this nor any other programme. No motor-bicycles, no aeroplanes nor motor cars. Silence so deep on a Sunday morning that you can hear the sheep nibbling if you live in the country and you can hear the church clocks three parishes away if you live in a town.

Now let us suppose you or I were children of the lower-middle, middle or upper-middle classes – that is to say, anything from tradesmen upwards – and that it is a Sunday morning 70 years ago: 1881. We are a very respectable family and, like almost all Victorian families, a large one: eight of us including Papa and Mama.

The first thing is that we get up a little later on Sunday, and outside it is unnaturally quiet: no carts and jingle of harness, no street cries, no noise of gravel being raked on the drive or of hedges being clipped. The world seems asleep under the Sunday sun. The cart horses are turned loose in the fields, the farm implements are glittering undisturbed, even the dogs are not barking.

We put on our best clothes. An elder sister today will wear that new dress, for church is the place to show it. Younger brothers will be in Eton jackets, elder brothers in tails. And as we all assemble for morning prayers in the dining room and Papa opens the Bible and the servants in clean black dresses and new caps sit in the chairs against the wall – as we assemble for our first worship, there is a crackle of new starch and slight smell of moth-ball.

The urn has been boiling for breakfast coffee all through prayers. After the meal comes almost the nastiest part of the day for the children. The younger have to learn their catechism; the elder have to learn the collect for the day from the prayer book. Half an hour before church they are assembled in front of Papa. Oh what heartburnings! Oh what stammerings! Oh what bitter words or beatings or punishments are meted out in various Italianate villas, sham castles and stucco terraces all England over in that fatal after-breakfast hour on Sunday morning!

And now, tears wiped away and a clean Eton collar on – to replace the one Papa seized in his wrath when for the third time you stumbled in the fourth commandment – you are ranged in your place with the rest of the family and you walk to church. From far and wide come other processions. Top hats are doffed and smiles exchanged. Or people look the other way, for in the genteeler suburbs of our towns there is much class distinction, and people in the wholesale way of business are distant with those in the retail trade, and professional classes – apothecaries, attorneys and the like – look down on any form of trade whatever.

Over chimney-pots and billowing smoke where servants cook the Sunday lunch, over trees and hedgerows call the bells, beautifully rung by teams of six or eight men whose delight it is to practise the old English art of change-ringing.

As for the church itself, the family will have its own pew with a visiting card slipped into a brass frame on it to show the pew rent has been paid if we live in a town or its pew established by custom if we live in the country. And woe betide a stranger who sits in a private pew. 'Excuse me, this is OUR pew.'

The service will be Morning Prayer, although at St Michael's, the high church in the poor part of the town, there are all sorts of bowings and scrapings of which Papa does not approve. Respectable families like Morning Prayer. The parson's black trousers show under his long white surplice. He wears an Oxford MA hood, slipping over one shoulder, and a very broad black scarf. And my word! – he preaches for a long time.

Every now and then it is Sacrament Sunday. Flagons and a silver cup appear on the Holy Table and the children are chased out halfway through the service, thankful to escape home without all the grown-up chatter that goes on during the walk back from church on an ordinary Sunday.

Wet or fine, winter or summer, Sunday lunch is always hot and it always consists of a large sirloin of beef and Yorkshire pudding followed by a fruit tart.

In the afternoon the boys go out for a walk. On rainy days the children must stay indoors. But no games are allowed. They may read *The Pilgrim's Progress* or that more thrilling allegory *The Holy War*. Perhaps in kindly disposed households with Tractarian leanings they may read the novels of Charlotte M. Yonge – *The Daisy Chain, The Little Duke, The Heir of Redclyffe* –

for although she is an entertaining and brilliant novelist, she makes up for those defects by being a Christian. Did I say no games are allowed? There are a few Sunday games: a spelling game with Bible texts and a sort of Happy Families with cards depicting famous missionaries.

There is also at some time in the afternoon Sunday school for the children. And oh what pretty girls teach in the Sunday school. And oh how much more the gentler side of our faith was learned in Sunday school than from the harsh admonitions of Papa or the wearisome sermons of the rector. The evening meal is cold to enable the servants to go to church. Evensong or Evening Prayer was always, as it still is in some of the more old-fashioned places, the popular service. Young couples went there together and courted on the way back in the lanes of a summer evening. In country districts 50 years ago the farm workers usually went to Evensong only, even though they had been confirmed. In some parishes it was believed that only squire and farmers were fit to take the Sacrament. 'Sacrament ain't for the likes of us.'

Those days are gone. The Victorian Sunday is gone. The chapels that did so much to bring a faith in Christ as the Son of God to the people are less well attended than they were in those days. Then the Church of England was 'respectable' and the other places of worship, whether Methodist, Congregational, Roman Catholic or Baptist, were thought not quite the right thing socially. This respectability very nearly killed the Church of England. But its great Victorians – Catholic, Liberal and Evangelical alike: Pusey, Kingsley, Simeon and later those martyrs for the Faith like Charles Lowder, Robert Dolling and Alexander Mackonochie – helped to make the Church of our country what it is today: a place where you go to worship your Creator and not for social convention.

Oh dear. I seem to have given the impression that most Victorian church-going was hypocrisy and that the Victorian Sunday was a miserable affair. Of course it was not. It was part of the life of our land. Its origin was Puritan, dating from those Reformers whom Queen Mary burned at the stake. It was their attempt to revive the Jewish Sabbath on a day when the people had leisure for recreation; to impose discipline on the fun and games of Catholic England's holy days which were getting somewhat out of hand. It was, as it were, the nationalization of leisure.

It survived, the Victorian Sunday, till lately. I can still remember when the old North London Railway did not run during church time. And to this day Sunday services of trains and buses are different, shops are shut, licensing hours vary, cinemas do not open till churches shut, and there is an atmosphere of partial peace. Sunday is, thank goodness, *different* and we must have one day in seven different or our nerves collapse, our way of living goes too fast and there is no escape from the machines that all but control us.

The Victorian Sunday was not just different. Those who remember it look back on it not wholly with loathing; some of them even look back on it with affection. Sunday then brought religion into life, even if it was only for one day a week and then rather boringly: Victorian children at least learned what the Christian faith was, even if they rejected it or ceased to practise it afterwards. Today most of us don't even know what it is we say we don't believe.

Sunday evening service from
St Michael's, Lambourn

BBC Radio, 28 September 1952

I am standing at the lectern of St Michael's, the parish church of Lambourn in Berkshire. Everyone who knows anything about racing has heard of Lambourn. Up here on the Downs are miles of gallops on springy turf and many famous stables. This church, in the midst of it all, is big and old and beautiful. If I had the time I should like to tell you about its age and its altars and tombs and brasses, the Norman bits, the hunting scene carved in one of the arches, the alabaster portrait of our Royal Martyr, Charles I. But I can't, for we are here taking part in an exciting experiment concerned with our church today. It is because of the present and not only of the past that we are here. And I am feeling unpleasantly like a parson, as there's a congregation sitting in the pews in front of me. And it's a large congregation. In a minute I will tell you why.

But before I do so, here briefly is why a practising Christian, whether he's a parson or layman, thinks differently from those who don't bother about religion. First he believes that extraordinary story which has persisted and grown in the last 2,000 years, and will eventually be known to everyone – that the Creator of the World became a man 2,000 years ago. Eternity came into time. All the ages before were a preparation for the birth of Christ at Bethlehem. Next he believes that if a man, or a nation for that matter, lives for himself, unhappiness, strife, and in the end disaster, follow. If a man lives for God, happiness, peace and joy is the result even in the course of hardship and suffering. A good many people think that is probably true, and they say, 'Oh, I live just as good and clean a life as so and so, but I don't go to church.' And the parson has to say to that, 'Very probably you do. But you're lucky. We have been told by Christ and his Church what to do to be given the strength to lead a Christian life. We must be baptized, confirmed, we must receive the Holy Communion, we must pray and study the Scriptures, and worship God every Sunday and big feast day.' And how on earth is a parson going to persuade people who think they're plodding along all right that they really must practise the faith into which they were, or were not, baptized, in order to find out why they were born and what they ought really to be doing, and how far they fall short of doing it? Most parsons are thought amiable idiots who have to be nice to everyone; as for what people believe, that's none of their business. But the truth is, of course, that until you make a point of going regularly to church and using its sacraments for at least a year – even if you think sometimes it is all a lot of nonsense – until you do this, you don't realize how different being a Christian is. It doesn't necessarily make one 'better' morally or physically. It's just different. It is not taking medicine to do oneself good. It is the art of giving oneself to God first and then to the neighbours.

It is difficult for priests – particularly country ones – not to become lazy or embittered or go mad with frustration seeing no results of their trying to make their parish think of religion as something more than being respectable. People are always ready to take offence: 'Oh he's too high! Oh he's too low! Oh I don't like his voice. Oh he's not as nice as old Rev. so and so was.'

The vicar of Lambourn, who is just behind me here in the chancel, has devised a way out. He talked to his friend the vicar of Ardington, another downland parish, at a diocesan clerical cricket match three years ago. He outlined a scheme. Then he asked the rector of West Ilsley and Farnborough, two very lonely downland villages, to join him. Eventually, six isolated downland clergymen who did not know much about one another formed this Downs Group, whose Evensong we're attending tonight.

First they met in one another's houses for one day every month for nine months. The visitors brought their picnic lunches, the host provided coffee and, in winter, soup. Then they all went to Mirfield together, which is a training college for priests, and spent three days in prayer away from the world. After nine months thinking, they formed a plan. First each vicar should visit every house in his parish. Then this would be followed by visits of all six incumbents' parishes one at a time. Two of the parishes have so far been visited. If you lived in either of those places, you could not avoid being called on by one of the Downs Group priests. Moreover, there was no chance of your fobbing him off with small talk. A letter would have come a week before, warning you he was coming and that he was going to talk about religion. The object of the visit was to get people who were churchmen in name to come to church again. There are seven more parishes to be visited.

It says a lot for the friendliness of the places so far visited, Lambourn and East and West Challow, that nowhere did the Downs priests meet with a rebuff. Here they are in the chancel behind me. Besides visiting their own parishes, they have so far visited about a thousand houses in their neighbours' parishes. The visits were a success. And I can see why. I wouldn't mind saying what I thought about religion, asking questions and explaining my own secret difficulties and wrongdoings, to a strange vicar. It would be with my own vicar I would wish to stand well. The result of these visits has been in each village an increase in church membership, the founding of a guild in one parish, the opening of weekday mission services in an isolated part of the parish of Challow.

But visiting was not all. An interchange of pulpits was arranged for Evensong, so that while you have your own vicar for the Sunday morning services, in the evening you get visited by the other five vicars in turn, who come to your parish to preach for three Sundays in a row. This visit is followed up by the return of your own vicar for the next three Sundays, and then one of the others will visit you, and so on.

Last of all, there are grand occasions like tonight. Outside the churchyard in the square there are many empty buses. They have brought the congregations from the other parishes in the Downs Group here to Evensong, because it is the eve of the feast of St Michael (Michaelmas Day is tomorrow), the patron saint of Lambourn church. Next time there is a patronal festival – on the eve of the day – the buses will be outside All Saints' Church, West Ilsley. A church is not just your parish church, it is the Church of England. Here at Lambourn you can sense that. It is not the vicars who make the churches. It is these people here in the pews. It is their prayers which are supporting these churches and bringing them to life. This service which is being broadcast would have happened anyway. But if we can have the help of your prayers as well, you who are listening to our friendly, country Evensong, we have yet more hope for bringing back the children of God to their Father. Pray for us.

On marriage

from *Moral Problems: Questions on Christianity with Answers
by Prominent Churchmen* (1952)

*As a married man in a job, what is the good of my becoming a Christian
when I can't possibly live up to Christ's ideal standard?*

To answer this question at its lowest level, one might say it is better to
have an ideal than no ideal at all. The person who marries without any
intention of keeping his marriage vows and who intends to leave his wife
as soon as he is tired of her body is not really marrying. He is satisfying
his body only.

Heaven knows it is difficult for many people to remain faithful. Their
wives may be unfaithful to them, or may turn into shrews or drunks
or bullies, or transfer all their affection to their children, or become
insanely jealous. The husband can be tempted almost beyond endurance,
for a man goes on being attractive to women for longer than most women
remain attractive to men. Advertisements, newspaper stories and most
modern novels incite us to adultery. We see many people who have made
a 'success' of a second marriage after divorce. From the worldly point of
view it looks as though there is every reason for breaking the chain of an
unhappy marriage.

I do not see how, without sacramental grace, it is possible for many
people to remain married in middle life. But they *do* remain married, and
in many households this is a miracle for which one can thank God. The
miracle always happens when both partners of the marriage, or even one
partner, are practising Christians who receive grace to keep their marriage
vows, first from the sacrament of marriage itself and then from the sacrament of Holy Communion. Despite lapses, a man may continue married
even if he is not happily married, by grace given to him in the sacraments
and in moments of stress by counsel of a priest and use of the sacrament
of penance. Thereby he is able to turn his eyes from himself and his
neighbours and to look up to God. And he has this consolation for his
lapses – that as Christ was God and Man and we are not God, we cannot
be perfect. But we can at least try to be perfect. The very fact of wanting

to follow Christ is something. One is given the strength to follow Him in the sacraments. That this is true any practising Christian will tell you, and will give instances.

Finally, when he is married a man is not alone. His wife's love helps him, whether he is a Christian or not. Even if at times that love seems to have disappeared, it is different from the love of a man. For it often goes on for longer and can sustain a marriage that seems to be broken. Tennyson at the beginning of his poem 'Romney's Remorse' quotes a passage from one of Edward Fitzgerald's letters which is an encouraging instance of love in old age, the time when love is truest, because it is stripped bare of flesh and the world: 'I read Hayley's Life of Romney the other day – Romney wanted but education and reading to make him a very fine painter: but his ideal was not high nor fixed. How touching is the close of his life! He married at nineteen, and because Sir Joshua and others had said that "marriage spoilt an artist" almost immediately left his wife in the North and scarce saw her till the end of his life: when old, nearly mad and quite desolate, he went back to her and she received him and nursed him till he died. This quiet act of hers is worth all Romney's pictures! even as a matter of Art, I am sure.'

I notice now that the questioner says he is a married man 'in a job'. I think the job, unless it is white-slave traffic or usury, or the like, is irrelevant to the question. But I hope it is not uncongenial. And an uncongenial job is less degrading to a man than none at all.

The power of prayer

The Spectator, 6 July 1956

I had always heard that Fulham Palace was rather a dull house. I suppose this was because I had always heard about it from clergymen and they rarely like Georgian. But I saw it for myself last week and can give the lie to any derogatory rumours. It is very hard to find behind blocks of flats and bushes and down a long lane off Fulham Palace Road. Go past a Gothic lodge and there is a courtyard of dark red Tudor brick, with diaper patterns in black glazed bricks. This leads to a Tudor hall which was much improved in the reign of George II and looks like a college hall, say that of Trinity, Oxford. The house itself which adjoins it was designed by S. P. Cockerell, the architect of Daylesford and Sezincote, Gloucestershire, and Banbury parish church. Cockerell designed it for dear old Bishop Howley, that splendid opponent of all 'progress' and devotee of landscape gardening, in 1814. Its garden front is of beautiful brownish stock brick with well-proportioned windows. In fact it is one of those subtle houses whose elegance is all in its proportion.

The reason I went to Fulham was a private party to hear the Mirfield Fathers Hugh Bishop and Trevor Huddleston appeal for sending a community of contemplative nuns to Basutoland. This is an area about twice as big as Wales where Europeans are not allowed to settle and entirely surrounded by the Union of South Africa. It is hard to explain the value of nuns whose lives are entirely prayer without sounding churchy, but as Father Huddleston pointed out, the political problems of Africa, and I would add of anywhere else, are in the end only solved by prayer. The nuns to go out are from the Society of the Precious Blood, an Anglican Order at Burnham Abbey, Bucks. This place has in my own experience caused what seem like miracles to happen when I have asked for its prayers about particular personal problems. Father Hugh Bishop gave an instance of his own experience. When he was a prisoner in the last war in Germany, at a particular time a lot of strange things started to happen in the camp. Many more people began to come to his services and to be instructed. An embittered Communist suddenly applied to him for baptism and became an unembittered and active Christian. When Father Hugh Bishop was repatriated he visited Burnham Abbey and happened to mention to the Mother Superior that he was a prisoner of war in Germany. She asked the name of his camp and then told him that at one period during the war, the same period as when the strange things happened in his camp, the nuns had asked that their prayers should be given to one particular camp, and the one which they had chosen had been his.

Vicar of this parish

BBC2 Television, 29 July 1976

One evening a hundred years ago, two people were talking in the village of Clyro, in the Welsh border country. One was the local curate, Francis Kilvert, then in his early thirties; the other was a remarkable old woman of 90 called Hannah Whitney.

She was talking of the two extraordinary sermons she heard preached in Llanbedr church by Parson Williams. 'He was a good Churchman,' she said, 'but he was a very drunken man.' 'How then,' said Kilvert, 'being a very drunken man could he be a good Churchman?' 'Oh,' she said, 'he read the lessons very loud, and he was a capital preacher. He used to say to the people in his sermons, "My Brethren," says he, "don't you do as I do, but you do as I say."'

Parson Williams was very quarrelsome, a fighting man, and frequently fought at Clyro on his way home from Hay. One night he got fighting at Clyro and was badly beaten and mauled. The next Sunday he came to Llanbedr church bruised black and blue, with his head broken, and a swollen nose and two black eyes. However, he faced his people and in his sermon glorified himself and his prowess, and gave a false account of the battle at Clyro in which he was worsted. He represented himself as having proved victorious.

The text was taken from Nehemiah 13.25: 'And I contended with them, and cursed them, and smote certain of them, and plucked off their hair, and made them swear by God.'

Another time he was to preach a funeral sermon for a farmer with whom he had quarrelled. He chose this text – Isaiah 14.9: 'Hell from beneath is moved for thee to meet thee at thy coming.'

That story is taken from Kilvert's diary. Thirty-five years ago nobody had ever heard of him, except members of his family and a few aged country folk or their descendants. Today there is no need to explain who he was, because after his diary got into print it was soon recognized as one of the best of all English diaries.

What Kilvert's diary does is to take us right into an out of the way country village in the 1870s, and I think there is no other book which gives quite such a detailed picture of what life was like in such places then. But the diary gives more than a picture; it creates an atmosphere, and evokes what would now be called a lifestyle. It's full of stories about other people, but it paints a self-portrait of a fascinating man whom we get to know with a special intimacy.

On a September day he walks to Llanthomas across country to tell a Mr Thomas, a clergyman, that he is in love with one of his daughters called Daisy and wishes to marry her. There is an awkward interview in the garden.

> Mr Thomas said I had done right in coming to him, though he seemed a good deal taken aback. He said also a great many complimentary things about my 'honourable high-minded conduct', asked what my prospects were, and shook his head over them. He could not allow an engagement under the circumstances, he said, and I must not destroy his daughter's peace of mind by speaking to her or showing her in any way that I was attached to her. . . . I felt deeply humiliated, low in spirit, and sick at heart, but I was comforted by remembering that when my father proposed for my mother, he was ordered out of the house, and yet it all came right. I wonder if this will ever come right. . . . On this day when I proposed for the girl who will I trust one day be my wife I had only one sovereign in the world, and I owed that.

That tells us two of the key things about Kilvert – that he had feelings and no money.

No small wonder he had no money: he was one of the six children of a country parson in Wiltshire who had to augment his stipend by taking in pupils. One of these pupils, in later life, wrote:

> Kilvert's father, the rector of Hardenhuish, near Chippenham, was ultra-Evangelical, a dry scholar, very hot-tempered, entirely without originality, and with no knowledge either of the world or of little boys. He punished his pupils, who were a set of little monsters, ferociously and unjustly for exceedingly slight offences; and living under this reign of terror they learnt nothing useful, and spent much time learning by heart the Psalms and the Thirty-Nine Articles.

The odd thing is that Kilvert later on looked back on this as what he called his 'sweet old home', so perhaps the rector segregated his sons from his pupils and gave them a less rough time.

From there, Kilvert went to a school near Bath kept by his uncle, another parson, and then up to Oxford. He was ordained when quite young, acted for a time as curate to his father in Wiltshire, and at the age of 24 went as curate to the vicar of Clyro in Radnorshire, the Reverend Richard Lister Venables. He was kind to Kilvert, as also was his sympathetic and understanding wife. The seven years Kilvert spent there seem to have been quite his happiest. People of both the landowning and the labouring class got as fond of him as he did of them, and he didn't find it easy to leave Clyro, which he did at the age of 31, and go back to Wiltshire. When he had just turned 37, he was presented to the living of Bredwardine, on the Wye in Herefordshire, not far from Clyro.

In spite of his lack of private means, Kilvert had no wish or intention to remain a bachelor, and at last, at the age of 38, he married a young woman called Elizabeth Rowland. She was 22, and he had known her for three years. They went off to Scotland for their honeymoon and returned to an affectionate welcome from his parishioners at Bredwardine in a downpour of rain. This saturated the triumphal arches put up for the occasion, but did nothing to dampen the presents and speeches, and the warmhearted villagers took the dripping horses out of the drenched carriage and themselves drew it to the vicarage.

Within a couple of weeks Kilvert was dead. He had died suddenly of peritonitis, no doubt the result of a ruptured appendix – those were the days before appendectomy. He was only 38, and the year was 1879. He was buried there at Bredwardine, and his young widow went home to Oxfordshire and her father, did good works in the parish, and lived on for more than 30 years. She had hoped to be buried beside him, but left her departure a little too long. Two maiden ladies had been inserted, one on each side of her late husband, so poor Mrs Kilvert had to be deposited in a distant extension of the churchyard.

That little contretemps might have provided a motif for an ironical poem by Hardy: and Kilvert, by the way, was born in the same year as Thomas Hardy – 1840.

Speaking of Hardy reminds me of a descriptive passage in Kilvert's diary, which may well be called Hardyesque. On a summer's day in 1873, Kilvert travelled up to a remote village in Radnorshire where a fête was being held.

While the athletic sports were going on, I wandered away by myself into congenial solitude for a visit to the ruined church of Llanlleonfel. . . .

The ruined church tottered lone upon a hill in desolate silence. The old tomb-stones stood knee-deep in the long coarse grass, and white and purple flowers nodded over the graves. The door stood open and I went in. The window frames and seats were gone. Nothing was left but the high painted deal pulpit bearing the sacred monogram in yellow letters. Some old memorial tablets bearing Latin inscriptions in remembrance of Marmaduke Gwynne and his family were affixed to the East Wall. The place was utterly deserted, there was not a sound. But through the ruined windows I could see the white tents of the flower show in the valley beneath. I ascended the tall rickety pulpit and several white owls, disturbed from their day sleep, floated silently under the crazy Rood Loft on their broad downy wings, and sauntered, sailing without sound, through the frameless east and west windows to take refuge, with a graceful sweep of their broad white pinions, in the ancient yew that kept watch over the church. It was a place for owls to dwell in and for satyrs to dance in.

It is long since the church has been used, though weddings were celebrated in it after it was disused for other services. There is a curious story of a gentleman who was married there. Some years after his marriage his wife died, and it happened that he brought his second bride to the same church. Upon the altar rails she found hanging the lace handkerchief which her predecessor had dropped at the former wedding. The church had never been used nor the handkerchief disturbed in the interval of years between the two weddings.

This evocation of a solitude shows how fitting it is that Kilvert's gravestone is inscribed with the words, 'He being dead, yet speaketh': through his diary he not only speaks, but speaks with a living voice.

When the diary came to light it was found to have been written in 22 notebooks, closely written in a conventional hand, with no margins, perhaps for economy's sake. It had apparently been kept continuously from January 1870, until five months before his wedding in 1879; but there were two large gaps, each of six months. The manuscript had been inherited by Kilvert's widow, and she is said to have destroyed the missing portions because she thought them too private and personal about herself. Not only about herself, perhaps. The first of them almost certainly contained some allusions to Kilvert's infatuation in Wiltshire with a handsome girl called Ettie Meredith-Brown. We also know she was handsome because we have a photograph of her and also a description of her by Kilvert:

> At 4 o'clock Miss Meredith-Brown and her beautiful sister Ettie came over to afternoon tea with us and a game of croquet. Ettie Meredith-Brown is one of the most striking-looking and handsomest girls whom I have seen for a long time. She was admirably dressed in light grey with a close fitting crimson body which set off her exquisite figure and suited to perfection her black hair and eyes and her dark Spanish brunette complexion with its rich glow of health which gave her cheeks the dusky bloom and flush of a ripe pomegranate. But the greatest triumph was her hat, broad and picturesque, carelessly twined with flowers and set jauntily on one side of her pretty dark head, while round her shapely slender throat she wore a rich gold chain necklace with broad gold links. And from beneath the shadow of the picturesque hat the beautiful dark face and the dark wild fine eyes looked with a true gipsy beauty.

For three months Kilvert and Ettie seem to have been closely involved, and then to have parted. Perhaps it was the same trouble about his 'prospects'. He tells us later that the parting occurred on 'a dark sorrowful winter's day, the 7th of December', and how he wandered about afterwards in 'the cold, desolate streets of Salisbury, sick at heart, with the tender loving despairing words of the last farewell ringing in my ears' as he still seemed to feel 'the last long lingering pressure of the hand and the last long clinging embrace and passionate kiss and the latest sorrowful imploring look and beseeching word, "Don't forget".

This entry in the diary perhaps escaped either the eye or the scissors of Kilvert's widow. We know from her photograph that Mrs Kilvert, however amiable she may have been, was extremely unlike a ripe pomegranate – she looks more like a good, sound, cooking apple. It seems probable that she didn't like either her husband's amorous confessions or the prospect of their being read by strangers. The second missing portion of the diary presumably contained an account of Kilvert's courtship and his engagement to herself, and it is disappointing not to have it.

After the printed diary had become famous, an old lady who had been brought up in what was already beginning to be called the Kilvert country – that is, the border region of Herefordshire and Radnorshire – and who had been alive in his time, was asked, 'And what did your family think of Kilvert?' 'I don't suppose they thought of him at all,' she rather snubbingly replied, 'after all, he was only the curate.' Only the curate! Now he is immortal, and they are forgotten.

There were legions of country curates in mid-Victorian days. It's a curious fact that when Kilvert was young, quite half the undergraduates at Oxford and Cambridge were reading for Holy Orders. Naturally mid-Victorian curates, like other human species, were of all sorts, and no doubt some of them were prim, priggish, or prudish. But people have extraordinary delusions about Victorian prudishness. It may surprise you to know that when Kilvert was at Weston-super-Mare in the summer of 1872 he took it for granted that one went into the sea with nothing on. 'There was a delicious feeling of freedom', he says, 'in stripping in the open air and running down naked to the sea, where the waves were curling white with foam and the morning sunshine glowing upon the naked limbs of the bathers.' Just try that at Weston-super-Mare this summer, and see if there isn't something to be said for 1872.

At Shanklin, a year or two later, things weren't quite so free and easy, and one day Kilvert suffered a slight mishap.

> Yesterday the sea was very calm, but this morning the bay was full of white horses. At Shanklin one has to adopt the detestable custom of bathing in drawers. If ladies don't like to see men naked why don't they keep away from the sight. Today I had a pair of drawers given me which I couldn't keep on. The rough waves stripped them off and tore them down round my ankles. While thus fettered I was seized and flung down by a heavy sea which, retreating suddenly, left me lying naked on the sharp shingle from which I rose streaming with blood. After this I took the wretched and dangerous rag off and of course there were some ladies looking on as I came up out of the water.

No doubt there were other mid-Victorian curates who kept diaries, and no doubt most of these were of very slight significance, full of ephemeral trivialities: most diaries are like that. I remember a typical entry from an ordinary diary, kept in the present century: 'Another miserable wet day, even wetter than yesterday. It is earnestly to be hoped that it will be less wet tomorrow.' Although it is almost impossible for an English diarist to avoid harping on the weather, Kilvert never wrote like that. Here, deliberately at random, are some extracts from pages of Francis Kilvert's journal, for the year 1871.

Thursday, 11th August.

Old John Bryant told my father today as they were discussing the war with Napoleon, that he remembered the news coming from France that the King's head had been cut off. He was a boy at the time, thirteen years old, helping to drain a field near Bull's Copse at Tytherton, and he heard the men with whom he was working, talking about the news. One of the men was Farmer George Bryant's father, already an old man then, and he was able to remember a story confidently told about an inn at Sherston, with the sign of 'Rattlebones'. Rattlebones was one of Oliver Cromwell's chiefs. In a battle, Rattlebones was so badly wounded in the stomach that all his entrails came pouring out. But Rattlebones found a tile and holding it against his stomach, kept his entrails in while he went on fighting. 'Well done, Rattlebones,' cried Oliver, 'fight away and I'll give you the villages of Sherston and Pinckney.'

Monday, 15th August.

Went to see the old soldier to talk to him about the war. He said the French were very kind to him when he was quartered in the Allied Army at a small village not far from Waterloo. There was often a good and friendly feeling between them, he said, and when they were on the field, he had often been on picquet duty less than 50 yards from the French sentries. He would call out 'Bon soir!' The Frenchmen would sing out in return: 'Will you *boire*?' Then they would lay down their arms, meet in the middle space, and drink together. Old Morgan believes, and believed at the time, that if they had been caught fraternizing, he would have been shot or hung.

Saturday, 8th October.

Heavy rain in the night, and in the morning, the mists had all wept themselves away. In the night the wind had gone round from the cursed East into the blessed West. All evil things have come from the East, always, the plague, the cholera, and Man.

Tuesday, 25th October.

At Maellswych Castle last week, four guns killed several hundred rabbits in one afternoon.

Friday, 25th November.
I had a literary talk with Farmer Lewis Williams about Byron, Wordsworth and Walter Scott, until Greenway knocked at the door to ask him to come and carry the pig indoors.

Thursday, 8th December.
Speaking of fairies, David Price, who understands Welsh, but little English, he said, 'We don't see them now because we have more faith in the Lord Jesus and don't think of them. But I believe the fairies travel yet. My sister's son, who works at the collieries in Monmouthshire, once told me he saw the Fairies dancing to beautiful music, sweet music, in a Monmouthshire field. Then they all came over a stile close by him. They were very yellow in the face, between yellow and red, and dressed all in red. He did not like to see them. He said they were the size of that girl or thereabouts and he pointed to a child of 11 who was blowing the fire. But I have never heard of ghosts and evil things to be seen on the Black Mountain. They say they are there, but I have been about it at all times day and night and never saw anything worse than myself.'

Friday, 10th February.
After dinner last night, Mr Venables, kindly anxious to cure my face ache, made me drink four large glasses of port. The consequence was that all night and all today, I have been groaning with a bursting, raging, splitting, sick headache.

Saturday, 22nd July.
Mrs Nott told me that Louie of the Cloggau was staying with her aunt, Miss Sylvester, an extraordinary being, partly a woman, and partly a frog. She cannot walk but she hops. Her head and face, eyes and mouth, are those of a frog, and she has frog's legs and feet. She never goes out, except to the Primitive Methodist chapel, and Mrs Nott said she had seen her, hopping to and from the chapel, exactly like a frog.

Friday, 14th July, St Swithin's Eve.
I dined with the rector, Mr Venables. He told me of the sermons which old Mr Thomas, the vicar of Disserth, used to preach. He would get up in the pulpit without an idea about what he was going

to say, and he would begin thus: 'Ha, yes, here we are. And it is a fine day. I congratulate you on the fine day, and glad to see so many of you here. Yes, indeed. Ha, yes, very well. Now then, I shall take for my text so and so. . . . Yes, let me see, You are all sinners and so am I. Yes, indeed.' And he would sit down.

Sometimes he would preach about 'Mr Noe'. 'Mr Noe, he did go on with the Ark, thump, thump, thump, and the wicked fellows come and say to him, Now Mr Noe, don't go on there thump, thump, thump, come and have a pint of ale at the Red Lion. There is capital ale at the Red Lion, Mr Noe. For Mr Noe was situated just as we are now, there was the Red Lion close by the Ark, just round the corner. Yes, indeed. But Mr Noe he would not harken to them, and he went on, thump, thump, thump. Then another fellow would say, Come, Mr Noe – the hounds are running capital, yes, indeed. Don't go on there thump, thump, thump. But Mr Noe, he never did heed them, he just went on with his ark, thump, thump, thump.'

Few diaries are worth printing, and very few indeed worth printing in full. What was left out of the printed version of Kilvert's diary was mostly trivial, repetitive, or judged not to be of special value. There are some entries in the diary, as printed, which seem to some excitable people disturbingly candid, and of course they imagine that the editor's omissions must have been of a scandalous or pornographic kind. Not at all: Kilvert had a great deal of innocence, and was no doubt well aware that if you write anything down you can't be sure who is going to read it.

Now why do people keep diaries? For a variety of reasons. Somebody in close touch with celebrities may well feel that what they do or say in private may be worth recording. A careerist may keep in his diary a proud and self-justifying account of the steps by which he has arrived at fame and fortune. But their motives can't be much like those of an obscure country curate in mid-Victorian England.

For whom would such a man as Kilvert be keeping a diary? Was it for the benefit of his descendants, if he should ever have any? In fact, he left none. Was it to re-read in his old age? But he died in his thirties. Was it because he had something sensational to record or confess? He made no such claim. Kilvert could not, I think, be called introspective or introverted, but he did once ask himself, in his diary, why he was keeping it. This is what he wrote:

Why do I keep this voluminous diary? I can hardly tell. Partly because life appears to me such a curious and wonderful thing that it almost seems a pity that even such a humble and uneventful life as mine should pass altogether away without some such record as this, and partly too because I think the record may amuse and interest some who come after me.

There is the point. Everyday life did not seem to him ordinary or humdrum; even what he called the humble and uneventful seemed to him 'curious and wonderful', therefore enjoyable. His responses to it were evidently more alert and sensitive than those of the people around him. He wanted to record it, to give it a lasting shape, to communicate it to others, to entertain them. This was the impulse of an artist.

What sort of man was Kilvert? His sensibility did not make him an aesthete or dilettante. He shows no knowledge or taste at all in architecture, painting, or music: one might say that his diary is about people in a landscape; and surely that is mainly what makes a good diary – human interest in a particular environment, and a zest for life in the diarist. Kilvert's social status was that of a poor clergyman, well educated but without money or social or ecclesiastical influence which might have advanced him. As a clergyman he was more than merely dutiful. In his time a country parish was still a close community; and as a parish priest he showed, to the best of his ability, care and sympathy for those who needed it, and affection too, and he was much loved.

His social and political views seem conventional and unquestioning, but while he mingles easily as a social equal with property-owning and professional people, he constantly visits the poor and afflicted. Except from hearsay he seems to have known little of industrial and urban miseries, but he knew when local people had no blankets or not enough to eat, and he minded, and tried to help them.

14 April 1871.
In the cross lane below Tybella old deaf Tom Gore was mending a ruined dry-stone wall. He said he had only one pair of boots in the world, they were cracked and full of holes and he had asked in vain of the relieving officer to beg the Board of Guardians to give him a new pair. He told me his wife was ill and he hoped he should not lose her.

He remembered that after he lost his first wife he often came home wet through to the skin, and no fire, and no food cooked. Four little children of his lay side by side in Bryngwynn Churchyard. He had seen trouble. He didn't know, but he thought it was his fate. He went on building up his stone wall at half a crown a perch. (That is more than sixteen feet.)

Kilvert didn't question the accepted ideas of the propertied class or express any doubts about imperial expansion: he was conventionally patriotic. His status, his opinions, and his religion evidently gave him a sense of security, or at least of continuity. If he had no money, at least he knew where his next meal was coming from; but every day he was in touch with people who knew nothing of the sort. A countrywoman whose mother had known and revered Kilvert once told me that when he had a chicken for his dinner he used to set aside half of it to take to some poor person who would be glad of it.

What did Kilvert look like? We have his photograph in profile. There he is, seated on a chair, wearing a clerical black frock-coat and floppy trousers, practical boots, a white bow-tie, and a thick dark beard which is virtually a mask. His thick, dark hair is shiny with pomatum, which the Victorians used to make with scented suet or lard. The camera may not lie, but it can anaesthetize a sitter, and the face is almost expressionless. The nose is short and straight; the eyes are averted from the camera, and appear small. He seems to have had some trouble with his eyes and was self-conscious about them. We know he had an attractive voice, and an old cousin of his remembered him as 'very sleek and glossy and gentle, rather like a nice Newfoundland dog'.

Kilvert was gentle, but not a softy; in fact he was a considerable athlete, not interested in sport, but a vigorous walker in the Welsh mountains. He had great energy and vitality. For most people, whether in Victorian or any other times, life is largely an endurance test, but Kilvert wrote in his diary, 'It is a positive luxury to be alive.'

It may have been but the situation of a young and healthy man with natural appetites, hedged in by the taboos of a non-permissive society, and in no position to live, like some Victorians, a double-life, even if he had wanted to. Kilvert had wanted to marry, in his Clyro days, Daisy Thomas, whose father turned him down. He was evidently headed off again from Ettie Meredith-Brown. So what became of him? He was in fact extremely susceptible, and was always in love with somebody. Richard Hoggart remarked that 'Kilvert had an enormous capacity for love in all sorts of aspects – for sensuality, for tenderness, for regard and affection . . . a sort of love flowed from his finger-ends.'

He was obviously attractive, in a magnetic sort of way, and knew it. 'It is a strange and terrible gift,' he wrote, 'this power of stealing hearts and exciting such love.' He did excite love and affection among all sorts of people, old and young, male and female, and notably in very young girls. Like his contemporary, Lewis Carroll, Kilvert doted on young girls. He idealized them, sentimentalized over them, and responded so warmly to their playfulness that even by present-day standards, he seems at times a shade indiscreet. If there had been anything sinister in his attentions to them he would hardly have written so candidly in his diary about his feelings. He could certainly have said, as Lewis Carroll once did, 'I am extremely fond of children – except boys.'

From his bedroom window in Clyro Kilvert had a view of a wooded hillside with a white farmhouse at the top, and when he looked up at it he used to think of a dairymaid who lived there. What he writes about her is half erotic, half religious; it is a sort of Pre-Raphaelite rhapsody:

> The sun looks through her window which the great pear tree frames and lattices in green leaves and fruit, and the leaves move and flicker and throw a chequering shadow upon the white bedroom wall, and on the white curtains of the bed. And before the sun has touched the sleeping village in the shade below . . . he has stolen into her bedroom and crept along the wall from chair to chair till he has reached the bed, and has kissed the fair hand and arm that lies upon the coverlet and the white bosom that heaves half uncovered after the restlessness of the sultry night, and has kissed her mouth whose scarlet lips, just parting in a smile and pouting like rosebuds to be kissed.

Such fanciful reveries are rare in the diary, which mostly tells of things seen and heard, not imagined. And the things seen are sometimes told with a beguiling innocence and a pure conscience. Here is a little mishap at a school feast on an August afternoon in Wiltshire:

> As we were swinging the children under the elms that crown the Tor Hill a girl came up to me with a beseeching look in her eyes and an irresistible request for a swing. She was a perfect little beauty with a plump rosy face, dark hair, and lovely soft dark eyes melting with tenderness and a sweet little mouth as pretty as a rosebud. I lifted her into the swing and away she went. But about

the sixth flight the girl suddenly slipped off the seat feet foremost and still keeping hold of the ropes she hung from the swing helpless. Unfortunately, her clothes had got hitched upon the seat of the swing and were all pulled up round her waist, and it instantly became apparent that she wore no drawers. A titter and then a shout of laughter ran through the crowd as the girl's plump person was seen hanging naked from the swing. O ye gods, the fall of Hebe was nothing to it. We hustled her out of the swing and her clothes into their proper place as soon as possible and perhaps she did not know what a spectacle she had presented. Poor child, I shall never see the elms on the Tor Hill now without thinking of the fall of Hebe.

Sexual frustration is apt to lead to sudden impulses which may or may not turn out happily if one gives way to them. In the summer of 1872, Kilvert was on his way by train to Liverpool to stay with some friends.

At Wrexham two merry saucy Irish hawking girls got into the carriage. The younger had a handsome saucy daring face showing splendid white teeth when she laughed, and beautiful Irish eyes of dark grey which looked sometimes black and sometimes blue, with long silky black lashes and finely pencilled black eyebrows. This girl kept her companion and the whole carriage laughing from Wrexham to Chester with her merriment, laughter and songs, and her antics with a doll, which she made dance in the air by pulling a string. . . . She had a magnificent voice and sung a comic popular air while the doll danced wildly. Breaking down into merry laughter she hid her face and glanced roguishly at me from behind the doll. Suddenly she became quiet and pensive, and her face grew grave and sad as she sang a love song. . . . The two girls left the carriage at Chester and, as she passed, the younger put out her hand and shook hands with me. They stood by the carriage door on the platform, then Irish Mary, the younger girl, asked me to buy some nuts.

Kilvert gave her sixpence and took only a dozen nuts out of a full measure. 'She seemed surprised and looked up with a smile. "You'll come and see me," she said coaxingly.' This led to quite a conversation, in the course of which the girls explained that they were hawkers, and Kilvert told Irish Mary that she had a beautiful voice.

A porter and some other people were looking wonderingly on, so I thought it best to end the conversation. But there was an attractive power about this poor Irish girl that fascinated me strangely. I felt irresistibly drawn to her. The singular beauty of her eyes, a beauty of deep sadness ... her swift rich humour, her sudden gravity, her brilliant laughter, a certain intensity and power and richness of life and the extraordinary sweetness, softness, and beauty of her voice gave her a power over me which I could not understand or describe, but the power of a stronger over a weaker will and nature. She lingered about the carriage door. Her look grew more wistful, beautiful, imploring. Our eyes met again and again. Her eyes grew more and more beautiful. My eyes were fixed and riveted on hers. A few minutes more and I know not *what* might have happened. A wild reckless feeling came over me. Shall I leave all and follow her? No – yes – no. At that moment the train moved on. She was left behind. Goodbye, sweet Irish Mary. So we parted. Shall we meet again? Yes – No – Yes.

No wonder people had been looking on wonderingly. And what would have happened if Kilvert had given way, as he might have done, to that wild reckless feeling and gone off with Irish Mary? One can't quite see him hawking nuts in the rain with two teenage girls, but there were stranger partnerships in mid-Victorian times. And what happened to Irish Mary? Who knows? This was something more than a passing fancy. Nearly two years later, on a spring day in Wiltshire, after visiting sick and old people in the parish, Kilvert writes, 'The evening has been very stormy and many old memories have come over me especially memories of sweet Alice of Llandovery and Irish Mary.'

The rich have their troubles and the poor their fun, but one is often struck in the diary by the contrast between the style of the leisured families and the troubles of the very poor. Kilvert was constantly asked out to dinners and picnics, croquet and archery parties at local houses; he was a welcome guest, and enjoyed himself, but most of his time was taken up with 'villaging', as he called it, walking all round the large and hilly parish to visit often remote dwellings, to comfort the old and the sick and the poor and the mad and the lonely. Their lives were often grim, and there are tales of suicides and murders.

Here we are in June, 1870. On a hot day Kilvert is with a well-dressed party in carriages, bound for a picnic in the Golden Valley: 'There was plenty of meat and drink, the usual things, cold chicken, ham, and tongue, pies of different sorts, salads, jam and gooseberry tarts, bread and cheese. Splendid strawberries from Clifford Priory. Cup of various kinds went round, claret and hock, champagne, cider and sherry, and people sprawled about in all attitudes and made a great deal of noise.'

And here is a visit to Lower Cwmgwannon to see the old madwoman, Mrs Watkins:

> While I waited in the kitchen, the low deep voice upstairs began calling, 'Murder! John Lloyd! Murder!' The madwoman's son led the way up the broad oak staircase into a fetid room darkened. The window was blocked up with stools and chairs to prevent the poor mad creature throwing herself out. She had broken all the windows, glass and all the crockery. She lay with the blanket over her head. When her son turned the blanket down I was almost frightened. It was a mad skeleton with such a wild scared animal's face as I never saw before. Her dark hair was tossed weird and unkempt, and she stared at me like a wild beast.

Country memories went back a long way. Kilvert was friendly with John Morgan, an old veteran of the Peninsular War, and used to help him to dig up his potatoes and to get his pension. And old Morgan would tell him anecdotes of that war long ago.

> He said he well remembered being in a reserve line at Vittoria when a soldier sitting close to him on the edge of a bank had his head carried off by a cannon ball which struck him in front of the throat. The head rolled along the ground, and when it ceased rolling John Morgan and the other soldiers saw it moving and 'playing' on the ground with a twitching of the features for five minutes after. They thought it so extraordinary that the subject was often talked over round the campfires as an unprecedented marvel.

Perhaps the longest memory at Clyro was old Hannah Whitney's. She as a young girl could remember sitting and listening to the talk of old people born at the beginning of the eighteenth century or the end of the seventeenth century. Sometimes they talked of the fairies in which they believed. Boys returning from market had to wear their hats round the wrong way lest they should be enticed into the fairy rings or led astray by the goblin lantern; and there was an old man who used to sleep and dance to sweet fiddles on the mill floor.

In the earlier part of the last century, before the Oxford Movement and evangelical revival had got under way, the Anglican religion had sunk, in some country places, into an extraordinary state of neglect. Kilvert now and then heard reminiscences of this: 'Crichton said that old Boughrood church was a most miserable place. The Choir sat upon the altar and played a drum.' Then in Dorset:

The Vicar of Fordington told us of the state of things in his parish when he first came to it nearly half a century ago. No man had ever been known to receive the Holy Communion except the parson, the clerk, and the sexton. There were 16 women communicants and most of them went away when he refused to pay them for coming.... At one church there were two male communicants. When the cup was given to the first he touched his forelock and said, 'Here's your good health, Sir.' The other said, 'Here's the good health of our Lord Jesus Christ.' One day there was a christening and no water in the font. 'Water, Sir!' said the clerk in astonishment. 'The last parson never used water. He spit into his hand.'

Kilvert was not pompous about his religion, and has some lively stories about mishaps or eccentricities in church, and about a remarkable hermit whom he calls the Solitary, and whom he visited. This was the Reverend John Price, a Cambridge man and vicar of an outlying parish, who lived alone in extreme poverty and squalor in a filthy hovel in a field: 'The squalor, the dirt, the dust, the foulness and wretchedness of the place was indescribable, almost inconceivable.' But he was received with great civility, and when they went out 'the people who met him touched their hats to his reverence with great respect'.

They recognized him as a very holy man and if the Solitary had lived a thousand years ago he would have been revered as a hermit and perhaps canonized as a Saint. At a gate leading into a lane we parted. There was a resigned look in his quiet melancholy blue eyes. The last I saw of him was that he was leaning on the gate looking after us. Then I saw him no more. He had gone back I suppose to his grey hut in the green. The evening became lovely with a heavenly loveliness. The sinking sun shot along the green pastures with a vivid golden light and striking through the hedges here and there tipped a leaf or a foxglove head with a brilliant green or purple.

Here is another moment with a religious flavour, a charming little story about a child:

> The Bishop of Worcester, who is singularly spare and attenuated, was staying in a house. He observed a child looking at him very attentively for some time, and when the Bishop left the room the child asked, 'Is the Bishop a spirit?' 'No, the Bishop is a very good man, but he is not exactly a spirit yet. Why do you ask?' 'Because,' said the child gravely, 'his legs are so very thin, I thought no one but a spirit could have such very thin legs.'

Kilvert was not always stuck in one place. He visits London, Oxford, the Isle of Wight, Cornwall, Bath and Bristol, and we know he visited Switzerland and France. In good repute among the local clergy, he was so well thought of at a higher episcopal level that he was offered the chaplaincy at Cannes, which seems an unusual preferment for an unworldly and inconspicuous country parson. His diary at Cannes, in what would then have been to him an unfamiliarly grand, worldly, and cosmopolitan society, would have been worth having, but his heart would not have been in it. Kilvert had lost his heart to the country people round Clyro and Bredwardine. Perhaps that was why he declined the offer.

A man so fond of people and of chronicling their sayings and doings is unlikely to be perfectly solemn, and there is a good vein of humour in the diary. There used to be a most delightful railway along the Wye Valley between Hereford and Brecon, and here is a delightful account of an old lady, Mrs Dew, making an outing by train from Whitney-on-Wye to Hereford and proving rather a trial on her son, a clergyman:

> At Whitney station Henry Dew and his mother got into the train to go to Hereford. They wanted to go second class but one carriage was full of farmers and another was full of smoke generated by the two captains, so they went first class and paid the difference. While Mrs Dew was standing upright in the carriage, the train snatched on suddenly, throwing her back breathless into her seat. The station master threw in a parcel of blankets after them and away they went, leaving on the platform a brace of rabbits which they were to have taken to the Frederick Dews. The rabbits were sent after them by the next train, but being insufficiently addressed and unable to find Mrs Dew they came back by the train following. Meanwhile Mrs Dew in Hereford had been much discomposed

and aggrieved because her sons Henry and Frederick would not allow her to spend more than an hour and a half at Gethin's the upholsterers', a time in which Henry Dew said he could have bought the whole town. He declared he never was so glad to get away from anywhere as from Gethin's shop where young Gethin and four shopmen were all serving Mrs Dew on the broad grin. Then Mrs Dew bought a large bag of buns and sweets for her grandchildren at Ayston Hill, the young Frederick Dews, but in the excitement of parting she forgot to leave the bag with them and brought it to Whitney. Then to crown all she was nearly driven over and killed by an omnibus in Broad Street. The omnibus came suddenly round a corner and she hollowed at the driver, the driver hollowed at her, the end of it being that she was nearly knocked down by the pole. Her son Henry saved her and told her she was not fit to go about Hereford by herself. She said she was. He said she thought she was ten years old and could go anywhere and was as obstinate as could be. While they were arguing, a cab came round the corner and nearly knocked the old lady down again. 'There,' said her son, 'there you go again. Are you satisfied now?'

Mrs Dew, by the way, had the unusual distinction of having been kissed by Coleridge when she was a baby. He is said to have almost smothered her with kisses: he said he had been wishing for a baby to kiss, which was the next best thing to bathing in the sea. She had the further distinctions of having had a sonnet addressed to her by Wordsworth, and of having broken off an engagement to one of Wordsworth's sons.

Throughout the diary there are exact and beautiful descriptions of landscape, and somebody has said that Kilvert's great virtue is the power of conveying the physical quality of everything he describes. He had the good fortune to live in parts of the English or Welsh countryside which had, and even still have, special beauties, and to be unusually aware of them. His England had its wrongs and its troubles but the countryside did have an intense and ancient quietness which has gone forever. Living before that horrible invention, the internal combustion engine, before the telephone, the radio, the aeroplane, and the pop festival, he experiences and continually fixes in words that marvellous, deep, lost peacefulness. If he had known that he was enjoying the great privilege of living in the last few remaining years of tranquillity he could not have taken more care to describe it.

Sometimes, on a quiet day in summer or autumn, the sort of day when any commonplace diarist would have felt that nothing whatever had occurred to write about, Kilvert would give a detailed account of what was to be seen or heard. Here is an example. April 1870. It is Easter Eve in Clyro church. People are decorating the graves with primroses and other spring flowers:

> More and more people kept coming into the churchyard as they finished their day's work. The sun went down in glory behind this dingle, but still the work of love went on through the twilight and into the dusk until the moon rose full and splendid. The figures continued to move about among the graves and to bend over the green mounds in the calm clear moonlight and warm air of the balmy evening. At 8 o'clock there was a gathering of the choir in the church to practise the two anthems for tomorrow. The moonlight came streaming in broadly through the chancel windows. When the choir had gone and the lights were out and the church quiet again, as I walked down the churchyard alone, the decked graves had a strange effect in the moonlight and looked as if the people had lain down to sleep for the night out of doors, ready dressed to rise early on Easter morning. I lingered in the verandah before going to bed. The air was as soft and warm as a summer night, and the broad moonlight made the quiet village almost as light as day.
>
> Everyone seemed to have gone to rest and there was not a sound except the clink and trickle of the brook.

By a complex of lucky chances, one man, evolved by a particular civilization, in a particular place and time, a man who had a healthy appetite for life and who was uncommonly articulate, left on record what he saw and what he enjoyed. By another tangle of lucky chances, we can escape into his lost world, now almost as remote as the world of a Chinese poem, though still just, just within living memory, and we can enter into it so closely that it seems to become part of our experience.

Once, on an afternoon in May, Kilvert had a sudden consciousness of that intense *joie de vivre* which makes his rather short and, as people used to say, uneventful life seem to us packed with brilliant events, and surprising scenes, and swarms of people, and intense feeling. An afternoon in May, and this was what he wrote in his diary: 'As I came down from the hill into the valley across the golden meadows and along the flower-scented hedges a great wave of emotion and happiness stirred and rose up in me. I know not why I was so happy, nor what I was expecting, but I was in a delirium of joy, it was one of the supreme few moments of existence, a deep delicious draught from the strong sweet cup of life.'

Part 5

BELIEF AND DOUBT

'I choose the Christian's way (and completely fail to live up to it)
because I believe it true and because I believe – for possibly a split
second in six months, but that's enough – that Christ is really the
incarnate son of God and that Sacraments are a means of grace and
that grace alone gives one the power to do what one ought to do.
And once I have accepted that, the questions of atonement, the Trinity,
Heaven and Hell become logical and correct.'

Letter to Roy Harrod, 25 March 1939

A sermon delivered at St Matthew's Church, Northampton, 5 May 1946

from *Five Sermons by Laymen*, 1946

Matthew 11.28. 'Come unto me, all ye that labour and are heavy laden, and I will give you rest.'

When I came into this church for the first time in my life, which was yesterday evening – coming in by that southwest door over there – I wanted to go down on my knees. For this is the sort of church which brings you to your knees. These soaring vistas of pale stone arches, the superb proportion of window to wall space, the delicacy of much of the detail from the profound, primitive simplicity of Henry Moore's *Madonna and Child* to the lace-like tracery of this beautiful wrought-iron chancel screen, the way the genius of Holding, the architect, leads your eye to the high altar there below the flashing jewels of the east window, that altar where the greatest mystery in the world happens Sunday after Sunday, and where, as we who try to be Christians try to believe, the Creator of the World, of the universe, of the trees and birds in the road outside, of the stones which Holding used to build the church, of the bones which help you sit upright in your seats tonight, where the Maker of our souls and minds, our very selves becomes present to hear our needs and answer our prayers in accordance with His Will – as I thought of all these things I did indeed want to fall on my knees and thank God for the beauty which man has made to the Glory of God in St Matthew's.

Then as I joined with you in worship at the great mystery of Holy Communion this morning, I realized that it was more than mere aesthetic beauty which made me want to kneel and which made me lower my voice as I entered the church last night. For this is a building which has been loved and prayed in. Your prayers, particularly at the Holy Communion, have soaked its stones in worship and have made St Matthew's a place where it is easy for a stranger to humble himself before God, to ask Him questions and to wait, in the reverent stillness of the congregation at the beautiful singing of 'O Lamb of God', for His answer. And I asked – what can I possibly tell these people, who come to church in such numbers, who have a beautiful building and the advantages of the full sacraments – what can I possibly tell them which will help? So please do not think of me as some special sort of person, a layman who is nearly a clergyman or any kind of expert in theology. I don't feel I ought to be in this pulpit. I would much rather one of you were here preaching instead of me. But since I *am* here, the best thing I can do is to expound my particular problems and what has helped me to solve them.

I feel sometimes that it is very hard to believe in God. And sometimes I envy those who have never had any doubt. I mean, I say to myself, can it really be true that nineteen hundred and forty-six years ago a child was born to a Jewish peasant woman, and this child was the very God who made the sun, the moon, the stars, this earth with me on it and all the spiders, alligators and everything else? And did this child grow to be a man, was He crucified, did He rise from the dead and send His Holy Spirit down to dwell in His Church? And there, where that light is twinkling through the iron screen in the Lady Chapel, nearly 2,000 years later, is that where He is Himself present in the form of consecrated bread and wine? When I worship with you at Mass I *know* it is true. And those moments when I *know* this is true remain in the memory so that doubt is dispelled. And because this is true, because the Creator of the World is present in this church and in thousands and thousands of others raised by the faith of so short a time as the last 2,000 years – because this is true, then nothing else is so important. Nothing else. Saints and far cleverer men than I have believed this, and so I will myself. It is no longer fashionable to be an atheist. And if it were not true, if the universe were an inexplicable accident, there is no point in anything. We would all have to go on living on this earth as long as possible, forever if we could, for there would be nothing afterwards. And if you read advertisements for medicines, breakfast foods and what not, you would think the people who write the lies about them really believed that we will live forever by gargling with TCP every night or eating Shredded Wheat in the morning. But you know and I know that somewhere in some builder's yard or at a saw mill or in virgin forest there is wood waiting and somewhere else screws are being made which will come together to make our coffins. To make your coffin, the coffin of the only person who is really you. And it is a very healthy thought – not a bit morbid – a very healthy thought, the thought of death. For it stops you worrying too much about those things of this world that don't really matter. Death makes me at any rate long to believe in God and to know, as we heard in the Gospel this morning, that He is the Good Shepherd.

But now here's the difficulty of a layman like me who has to work for his living. And I expect it is the same for most of you. The world is too much with us. Last week I heard the parliamentary secretary of the Ministry of Education make a speech. He said there was a cultural breakdown in Europe. Cultural breakdown! There's more than that. We live in mechanical barbarism, not in civilization at all. Nearly all of us are doing jobs which take up too much time so that we cannot get home, our wives are worked off their heads and are too tired to be cheerful when they see us. We earn money in office or factory simply to earn the right not to have to work *all* our lives. Our work is either too manual or too much office work. Our lives are unbalanced. He is either a very lucky man or a man wholly deadened by the social system who has a job today which gives him so much pleasure that he looks forward to returning to work after a holiday.

Think of the man working on a chain belt. Poor feller! He tightens a nut as it comes along on the belt. He gets adept at this and in case he should go mad or become careless, he is now and then allowed to tighten another sort of nut by way of variation. He will probably be doing it all next week to the accompaniment of music while he works and possibly his wife may be working somewhere else while the children are farmed out in a community crèche to play with the psychological toys. And when the day is over the man will bicycle back down treeless roads to his sleeping box and his food will come out of a tin and his music will come out of a wireless set and his opinions will be given to him in the newspaper. We let machines run our lives. We listen but we do not sing; we read, but we do not write; we feel, but we do not think; we buy, but we do not make; we judge things by money standards because money buys us escape from the roaring lunacy around us. We escape to see games which we do not play, towns where we do not live; lives, in screen and play, which are not our own. We escape from one vacuum into another. 'Come unto me, all ye that labour and are heavy laden, and I will give you rest.'

And here comes the point of all I have been saying to you. 'Come unto me, all ye that labour and are heavy laden, and I will give you rest.' That does not mean a rest in a deck chair when the grass is mown or a rest by the seaside, it means the true rest in the Lord. It means the faculty for not being worried by the world, for being able to distinguish good from evil; it means the calm of those really good people you know and everyone of us here can think of one or two among our friends or relations.

There is only one way of finding this true rest and that is by prayer. Let me make a suggestion to you, and forgive me as a layman for making it.

Supposing every day this coming week every person here goes into a church, this church if you like, and kneels before the altar or before the Blessed Sacrament where our Lord lives more intensely than anywhere else. Ask for the faith to believe that He is there, put yourself into the presence of the Creator of the World who loves you by saying 'In the Name of the Father and of the Son and of the Holy Ghost'. Wait and listen. All kinds of things may distract you: people talking; an argument going on in your head; the thought of some lying advertisement; buses changing gear outside; aeroplanes roaring; gradually a silence will be caverned out of the noise and you are in the Presence of God. Even if you can't believe this, go and try, the effort to believe will help you. And then say the Lord's Prayer slowly three times. Once thinking of your friends, once thinking of your enemies, once thinking of all those in the world who are doing disinterested acts of kindness in their fellow creatures whether they are Christians or not.

Then when you have done this each day for a week, you will want to do it for another week. It should not take you more than five minutes a day. Believe me, this is the way to find true rest, the real calm sense of proportion in this roaring world where we are watching the slow change-over from the agricultural to the industrial age. God's time is not our time. Do not worry about that. He will settle your problems for you, if you listen to Him and pray. And while you are about it, thank God for the priests and people who keep His churches alive. There where the light twinkles in the Lady Chapel and daily on the altar our Lord says, 'Come unto me, all ye that labour and are heavy laden, and I will give you rest.'

This I believe

CBS Radio, 21 September 1953

About 500 words – it is very difficult to tell you in so few words why I was born, what I am meant to do on this earth and why I am a member of the Church of England which is the same as the Episcopalian Church of America and part of the great Anglican branch of the Catholic Church throughout the world.

'I believe in God the Father Almighty, Maker of Heaven and Earth, and in Jesus Christ His only begotten Son Our Lord,' as we say in the Creeds, and I don't mind saying that I find this very hard to believe. I often ask myself, 'Can it really be true that the force that created these fingers of mine, which are holding the bit of paper from which I am reading to you, and also made the stars and the universe, cares in the least for me or what I say, let alone for the few remaining hairs on my bald head?' Yet if it isn't true and if we are all the result of a blind accident, then I think I would want to cut my throat or rush off and indulge myself in every physical excess of which my body is capable. But then I am asked to believe something much more difficult, and that is that God the Son, 2,000 years ago, became Man in the womb of a Jewish virgin in Palestine. Eternity became part of time in this simple way. If it is true then everything in the world, whether you believe in evolution or whether you don't, led up to that supreme moment of the birth of Christ and everything since that date leads away from it. How right are we to date everything before Christ BC and everything after him AD. I *want* to believe that Christ was God become Man. If that is so, then the resurrection, the sacraments of the Church, prayer and the Scriptures are comprehensible. If it is not true there is no point in everything; my own prayers that I have found answered, my own sins that have found me out, grace that comes to me in the sacraments and particularly when I receive Holy Communion, are all delusions: the huge cathedrals, the many priests and ministers and millions of Anglicans, our Anglican monks and nuns as well as priests and ministers of other churches and chapels are all deluded.

But of course it is true. I have seen people die secure and believing that they are cared for and loved by God become Man; I have sat by deathbeds and I know that the Christian religion is true. I know that there is a world beyond this one that is all round us, that good and evil spirits are fighting here among us and that here we are born into this battle between good and evil – which is another way of saying that we were born in original sin. And I hope that when I die I shall understand more of the purpose of God. He hides much from me now because my finite brain would not be able to understand it.

I do not believe that human nature is capable of perfection on this earth. I do not believe that bigger is better, nor that doctors will ever be able to take death away from us. I believe that love and not atomic energy is the most powerful thing on earth. I know that my own Church is full of love – or charity as we call it – and I believe that it is the true Church. I know that Christ, who was Perfect Love, lives in it. I force my will to make me believe that God became Man nearly 2,000 years ago. Lord, I believe. Help thou mine unbelief.

Christmas

The Country Churchman, December 1957

Vicars ought to write about Christmas, not laymen like me. And when the editor asked me to write, my first thoughts about Christmas were rather uncharitable. Forgive me if I put them down, but you may have shared some of them. Christmas cards, for instance – they only started about a century ago and were meant to be friendly messages between relations and old friends. Still one gets a few Christmas cards which are really meant and which serve as a letter to remind us that an old friend still thinks of us. But mostly Christmas cards have become a huge com-mercialized racket. London firms whose directors I have never met and who have never enjoyed the paltry custom I could offer them seize the opportunity to use the birth of Christ as an advertising campaign. Then there are those people who send us cards with illegible signatures and no address or only a Christian name, 'With best wishes from Mollie'. Which Mollie? And does the other Mollie spell it with a 'y'? The anxiety keeps me awake. The guilt mounts and by the time Christmas Day arrives there are nearly always one or two people in my mind I think I may have offended through not sending a Christmas card.

Then comes the anxiety about presents. These are meant to be expressions of love. But how often they become sources of worry. 'Will she notice that my present this year is not so expensive as last year's?' 'Had I better leave the price on?' 'Why did they send us a present this year when they know we never send them one?' And then there is that embarrassment of sending on a present one didn't want to some-body else and the original giver sees it: 'Oh, I gave one of those to the Betjemans.'

To continue these uncharitable thoughts, Christmas Day comes and to those who do not go to church it is just the first of a succession of Sundays. On Boxing Day people are a little livery through having eaten too much the day before. On the day after that the children are thoroughly out of hand and have lost interest in their new toys and smashed some of them. The presence of the husband in the house for so many days means that his wife is feeling the strain and that as the weather is too bad for him to

173

get out of doors he has taken to a little home carpentry and done untold damage.

All births are attended by anxiety, and I suppose it is only natural that the most important birth in the world, the birth of the Son of God, should be accompanied by these little difficulties that I wrote about in my uncharitable mood. But if you come to think about it, Christmas is the greatest cause for thanksgiving that we have. At that time about 2,000 years ago Eternity came into the world. God was made man, and that is why we kneel in that part of the Creed. We can't believe God became man without faith, and we don't have to be very clever to have faith. In fact, it is far harder to have it if we are clever; there are so many arguments against so unlikely a story. But there are far more arguments in favour of it, and some of them we see at Christmas when we go to church and receive Holy Communion, when we remember old friends and have our families round us, and there is more love going about than at other times of the year, when even the most crusty and ill-tempered of us break into a smile. But it all seems to me quite pointless to have these family reunions, holidays, and present-givings crowded into the end of December if we don't think Christ was God.

> And is it true? For if it is
>   No loving fingers tying strings
> Around those tissued fripperies,
>   The sweet and silly Christmas things,
> Bath salts and inexpensive scents
> And hideous tie so kindly meant.
>
> No love that in a family dwells,
>   No carolling in frosty air
> Nor all the steeple-shaking bells
>   Can with the mighty truth compare –
> That God was Man in Palestine
> And lives today in Bread and Wine.
>
> If there's no Truth on Christmas morn,
> Then why were any of us born?

Death

The Country Churchman, April 1958

I think about death every day of my life. I do not think it is morbid to do so but natural. I have got to die and I had better be prepared for it. So when I am in bed at night, I try to imagine this is my last moment on earth. Sometimes I am frightened and think, is there a God who loves me? And if there is, then I have done very badly and lived a licentious life and a hypocritical one and when I come to the judgement and my soul stands naked before my creator I shall be sent to hell, and what is hell like? Huge centipedes crawling towards me to sting and me not able to move? And then I think perhaps there is no life beyond the grave and no God and the promises of Christ are not true and I think I would rather hell than extinction and anyhow I am going away alone, as alone as I came into the world.

But these are only my gloomiest thoughts. Most of us have doubts sometimes whatever our religion, even if we are devout atheists. I have seen a good deal of death and when you are near someone who is dying it is not frightening but awe-inspiring – the faraway look in the eyes, the patient smile as the person turns to you coming back to earth for a moment, almost unwillingly, it seems. And then when they are dead their body is no longer them but something they have used: 'A worn out fetter that the soul has broken and thrown away', to quote Longfellow. Not that I want to suggest that the soul has nothing to do with the body. The resurrected body will be the way we will recognize one another as the disciples recognized Christ after His resurrection. But how this happens is still a mystery.

Death! I hope and pray that when I die I will be so full of love for God, so certain of his mercy, so sure that his sayings are true – 'Lo, I am with you alway, even unto the end of the world', 'In my Father's house are many mansions: if it were not so, I would have told you' – that I will look forward to leaving this world and meeting a loving merciful father. There are plenty of happy deaths like this. Only last year I was talking to an Anglican nun who had only a few months to live. 'Dying,' she said, 'is like packing up one's things at the end of term, very exciting.' She died in great peace last November and in her last days the mother superior told me her cell was the happiest place in the convent. Of course I know what to do. The Church of England in which I was born and brought up and in which I hope to die, as did that nun, can teach me by the Bible, prayer and the sacraments. But I wish I had the courage and strength to keep its rules. I hope and pray that everyone who reads this dies happily at peace with mankind and in love with God. That was how that nun died – and so have many people I have seen whose lives may well have been nothing like so good as hers.

The story of Jesus

Introduction to a Methuen Talking Book, 1960

This Talking Book tells the story of Jesus Christ in the words of the Bible. Of course, it cannot give you all the details as there is not room, but it sets out the main facts of the life of Jesus of Nazareth, the son of Mary and Joseph the carpenter, who was born about BC 6, in Bethlehem, and was crucified about AD 29 in Jerusalem. Out of that short life there arose the greatest religion the world has ever known, and this little book attempts to relate this life to the religion and the point of view that Christianity actually is. For the point of Christianity is Christ, a man who claimed to be the Son of God, and who lived and died as a man at a specific time and place. Therefore this book stresses especially the divine aspect of that man – a belief that Christianity holds to be the Incarnation.

Whether you are a Christian or not, Christianity is the background to our lives, as it is the basis of the western world. But this presents difficulty when we read the Bible, for we tend to forget that the words of the New Testament, loaded with associations for us, actually describe certain events that happened in a province of the Roman Empire on the eastern seaboard of the Mediterranean about 1,950 years ago. These events actually took place – 'was crucified under Pontius Pilate', the Creed says. And it says this so that we can get a fairly exact date, and modern scholars now place the crucifixion around AD 29. But unfortunately, to the men who wrote the Gospels, this kind of factual information for the most part seemed irrelevant; for example, we have no contemporary description of what Jesus looked like. These writers were struggling only to make out what it all meant, to stress those details that seemed most significant for them from what they remembered or had been told. The Gospels were all written within 80 years of the death of Christ, yet by modern standards as factual biographies they leave out much that we would consider important. But still, the facts are there and can be arranged without great difficulty into a sequence that makes sense.

To begin with, these events took place in Palestine where the land and the people have changed little in 2,000 years. Palestine is about the size of Wales; there is a green and fertile belt running along the eastern coast of the Mediterranean that spreads out in the north towards the Sea of Galilee; but in the south and the east, the land rises to a high plateau, barren and rocky on which is built the city of Jerusalem. Says the Psalmist, 'I will lift up mine eyes unto the hills, from whence cometh my salvation' – for Jerusalem was the sacred religious capital of the people chosen by God – the Jews – who inhabited the land.

Now all this land, the land of Israel, was part of the Roman Empire and had been for years. It was divided as the map shows into a number of provinces, and in fact Roman rule allowed the Jews to run these provinces very much as they liked; and at the time of the birth of Christ, Herod the Great was King of all Israel, under the authority of Rome. But this was not a new situation; for many centuries the Jewish nation had been in captivity or their land overrun by conquest from the east and the west – the Egyptians, Assyrians, Philistines, Babylonians, Persians and Romans had all at various times been their masters, and for as long as we have record, the Middle East – the meeting point of East and West – has been the centre of political trouble and intrigue as it is today. But out of this confusion over their native land, the Jews held fast to one central tradition, namely that God had a personal interest in them. This belief in and worship of one God – not in gods as their pagan conquerors – kept them united over the centuries; and part of the belief lay in the hope that God would send them a Messiah who would in the end lead them out of bondage and vindicate them forever. The story of this Messiah begins with the Annunciation of his coming birth to his mother Mary in Nazareth, a village in the province of Galilee.

But it is one thing to believe in the coming of a Messiah for many centuries and quite another to have it occur. Strange prophets and men with visionary gifts were often appearing out of the Judaean wilderness, to cause a nine days' wonder, and doubtless many thought of John the Baptist as just such a visionary when he announced that the Messiah was now truly at hand. But the story of the baptism of Jesus by John is described in such a way as to show us that this time something different had happened. It is fruitless to ask whether an actual dove descended, as it is to speculate on the Virgin Birth or the miracles. The only argument against any miracle is its intrinsic improbability. But if material standards are the only calculus, all spiritual events are of their nature, without exception, impossible. To the onlookers, at any rate, something New had occurred, and this was straightaway confirmed by what this New Man proceeded to do.

It was customary in the local synagogue – a combination of village hall, school and church that was the central institution of village life – for suitable people to be asked to read from the Scriptures, i.e. the books of the Old Testament, and to expound its meaning. Now this man, as the record tells us, implied that he *was* the Meaning, that the preparation of which these sacred books bore ample witness had now been fulfilled in him, that he was indeed 'he that should come'.

His implicit claim was to be the Son of God. This claim in fact was so appalling – as it still is – that after the natural initial incredulity, only two courses were left open: acceptance of that which can scarcely be apprehended by human intelligence, or outrage at an insane blasphemy. And indeed it is characteristic of the subtlety of Jesus' ministry that he never makes such a direct claim, but only behaves or speaks in ways that finally provoke people to say it of him.

Jesus' public ministry lasted at the most two years, and it reveals a consistent method: he was out to shock people into paying attention. For it may be asked what else is the point of the miracles? A gift of healing is an attractive accomplishment though it does not make a man God; but it does make people take notice. And then after this, to differentiate himself still further when people expected more miracles, more signs and greater wonders, he uttered yet another blasphemy – this time, he declared, he would *forgive the sins* of the man who had been brought to him to be cured of the palsy. For 'who,' said the people, 'can forgive sins, but God only?'

Such words and deeds would indeed gain attention and even notoriety. So he then begins to put forth a new kind of teaching; he talks about the Kingdom and the kind of people who shall enter and inhabit it. But it is not the sort of kingdom that would come first to the mind of an oppressed people, chafing under an imperialist rule. In fact it has nothing to do with a temporal kingdom at all, for it is a kingdom open and available to all; it is the kingdom within; it is a man's spiritual state and not his earthly habitation; and the sorts of people who have access to this, to whom it belongs in fact by right, are those he names in the Beatitudes in the Sermon on the Mount. And what a list it is! 'Blessed are the poor in spirit' – i.e. those whose lives, in worldly terms, are of no account whatever. 'Blessed are they that mourn' – i.e. those whose lives are desolate by the deprivation of the one thing that makes life worth living, the death of those we love. Indeed the first and most terrible thing about Christianity is its brutal lack of compromise. On this it is quite consistent. 'He that findeth his life shall lose it: and he that loseth his life for my sake shall find it.' And the whole recorded life of Christ is a parable on this theme, for it repeats again and again one lesson: if one continues to endure the tribulations that living life fully and thoroughly inevitably involves, the Kingdom is there for you – whether you think of it as a Heaven in the next world, or as a state that is grown and nurtured inside a man as the grain of mustard seed that becomes 'greater than all herbs'.

For the parable was Jesus' chief means of teaching: only at times does he directly reprove or exhort, and all his teaching about the spiritual world is by using only everyday things and matters for an example. In this way, people should first recognize the things he was talking about, and secondly they would have to think out the application of the parable for themselves; and to get a point home about things that are not of this world, an apt parable, neither too loose nor too precise, is the most perfect method yet devised.

As Jesus' ministry developed and came to a head, he seems to have limited his public activity in order to concentrate more intensively upon his chosen disciples, who were to continue his work after his death. We gather from the gospel that Jesus and the disciples went on two long preaching journeys: one up through Galilee as far as Sidon on the coast, and the second northeast over Jordan, towards Mount Hermon. At the end of this second mission, which might have lasted several months, the first person takes the first leap – Peter declares Jesus to be the Christ, to be, in fact, God. And eight days later, on the summit of Mount Hermon, the culminating spiritual event of the ministry occurs; the Transfiguration was apparently meant to confirm Peter's declaration. For a brief time, Jesus himself took on the vesture and the bearing of the God Peter had said he was; the spirit was permitted perfectly to shine through. From the description it was apparent and evident to those who saw him transfigured that the light in God had become a man; that, with the eye of faith, they had witnessed Incarnation. But the implications of this event were still to come in the next few weeks.

For Jesus then 'stedfastly set his face to go to Jerusalem', and Jerusalem is where the critical events of Christianity took place. He determined to go there at the time of the central festival of the Jewish year, the Passover, when the Jews gathered together to celebrate their liberation from bondage in Egypt. Amongst a strongly religious people this was the main event of the year, and Jerusalem would be packed for the ritual sacrifice of the lamb as a thanksgiving to God.

However much rumour or notoriety had spread abroad about this New Man out in Galilee or Jordan, it was still possible for the chief ecclesiastical authority in Jerusalem to cast a blind eye; a new prophet out in the backwoods was not such an uncommon phenomenon and would surely peter out. But Jerusalem contained the Temple, the Holy of Holies, the most sacred repositories of Judaism, and it was here that Jesus had to challenge the accepted order, and the accepted order was constituted by the Pharisees, the Sadducees and the Scribes – the establishment of Israel. The Pharisees and the Scribes represented an aristocratic and insular clique devoted to the meticulous observance of religious ritual and to the exposition of the law. The Sadducees, their rivals, were a more political though still religious group on friendly terms with Roman authority. Furthermore, at this time the province of Judaea, of which Jerusalem was the capital, was in the charge of a Roman Procurator, Pontius Pilate, as the previous Jewish Governor, Archelaus, a son of the late King Herod the Great, had been deposed for his irresponsibility.

Against this political background, it is thus quite clear why Jesus was crucified. He was condemned to death by crucifixion – a death reserved for only the lowest class of criminals, for slaves and never Roman freemen – as a political measure by the ruling class, on a charge of blasphemy; for on the one hand they feared that his popularity and authority would overthrow their own power, or that disruption and anarchy might overwhelm Israel. By their lights, it can be argued that they did their best for Judaism. But unhappily in life, there is no excuse for not acknowledging the Truth when one sees it. Jesus' entry into Jerusalem at festival time was a direct threat to the religious and political stability of Israel. He was tried on the charge of claiming blasphemously to be the Messiah – the King of the Jews – a claim, as the texts demonstrate, that he took the greatest pains to avoid making explicit, though he conducted himself in such a manner as to compel his detractors to use this title; for this he was condemned.

But though the Jewish religious courts found him guilty, the death sentence could only be imposed or ratified by a Roman court. Thus Pilate's acquiescence was vital. On our record we have been unable to include the trial of Jesus before Pilate; but at the outset, Pilate is disinterested enough to protest Jesus' innocence. It is only later, when he sees the expediency of maintaining good relations with the highest Jewish authority, that he washes his hands of the affair and gives in to their insistence upon the death penalty.

But we have here centred upon the crucial personal events of Jesus' last days on earth, the events of Holy Week which are called Christ's Passion. The Last Supper, the Agony in the Garden, the Betrayal by Judas Iscariot and the Flight of the Disciples, the Crucifixion, the Burial and the Resurrection, the episode of Doubting Thomas, and the Ascension.

These things, of course, are familiar as stories and our record recounts them; but how, in fact, are we to interpret the Passion of Christ? On one level there is nothing to be said at all, for nothing can be *proved*. But certain claims are put forward: briefly, a man who was the Son of God allowed himself to endure the most humiliating and painful execution, when he could quite easily have avoided this outrage, to atone for the sins of man against God, his Creator; furthermore, to effect a bridge between God and man by God becoming a man, and by taking on himself, in this midway position, the weight of mankind's misery. The claim is both stupendous and, in the last resort, incomprehensible, as our words are only a shadow of matters that are spiritually mysterious. The Last Supper, on one level, is a meal Jesus and his disciples took together, at which Jesus made certain statements about the bread and the wine that he had blessed and given them to eat. But what does 'This is my body' and 'This is my blood' actually mean? Various branches of Christianity construct differing and elaborate systems upon these very words, wherein some claim that the Mass and Holy Communion is not only a re-enactment of the Last Supper but an actual re-crucifixion of Christ, in a spiritually real sense, whenever the bread is blessed and broken – as Christ's body, in fact, was broken; others claim that such a ritual, again based on the Last Supper, is only an act of remembrance of the universality of Christ's Passion. Nevertheless, in Jerusalem AD 29, *something happened*, and whatever it was, the history of the world was henceforth changed; and from this happening there springs the great structure of Christianity.

But on the simplest level, as Keats said, a man's life of any worth is a continual allegory, and Christ was indeed such a man, a unique man, and the life, death, and resurrection of Christ are the perfect allegory of what happens to a man's selfhood when he attempts to love, that is, to live selflessly. He is, in some manner, crucified, and a new man is resurrected with his life now no longer directed towards what he can get out of it but based upon what he can put into it. And in a richly developed life, this is in fact what happens; but there will be few who will be so foolish as to deny that such a life is often painful. And the Passion of Christ, the man who was God, was exactly that.

Christmas from St Martin's

St Martin's Christmas Matinée, 1960

I do not see how it is possible to write about Christmas in a church paper, even so secular a one as this, without either preaching a sermon or rambling into rather arch belles-lettres. As a frequent exponent of the latter I prefer this time to try the former. It is difficult for me to preach because I am not a clergyman and find it no easier to believe than do other people. However badly one behaves and however much nastier one finds oneself than people who don't go to church (and this goes for the majority of my real friends) I suppose the vital fact about being a Christian is believing that Christ was God. This is very difficult, and in moments of despair or thorough enjoyment of some delicious self-indulgence I sometimes think that I have been hoodwinking myself and listen avidly to arguments disproving the truth of Christianity. And then at other times I am quite sure that Christ is God and why I am sure God only knows.

After all it is asking one to believe a great deal. We know the world is millions of years old and that human life on it is a good many thousands. Yet if we are Christians we are asked to believe that a baby born in a small tribe which has subsequently spread and shown itself very good at business was the Creator of the world. And this happened only 2,000 years ago. The Cornish poet, Hawker, thus describes Our Lady with God in her womb:

> She stood the Lady Shekinah of Earth
>   A chancel for the sky,
> Where woke to breath and beauty God's own birth
>   For men to see Him by.
> Round her too pure to mingle with the day
>   Light that was life abode;
> Folded within her fibres meekly lay
>   The link of boundless God.
> So linked, so blent, that when, with pulse fulfilled,
>   Moved but that Infant hand,

> Far far away the conscious Godhead thrilled
> And stars might understand.

This baby had to be washed, dressed and fed, and as He grew up was subject to just the same temptations to delicious self-indulgence as the rest of us. He was subject to misunderstandings, too, right from the start. You cannot really blame the people at the inn for turning out the holy family: they did not know the baby was the Creator of the world. You cannot really blame the soldiers for crucifying God as they did not know either, though I have a shrewd suspicion that Caiaphas, the high priest, knew exactly what he was doing and that Pilate thought there might be some truth in Jesus's claim, but like a good civil servant was taking no chances.

But we do know that the baby was God or at any rate most of us have been told that He was. And I don't see how a more simple way could have been invented for making the vast incomprehensible Mind behind the universe something that all stupid and even some quite clever people can understand. You could not really have a more generous present than the gift of God Himself. It is quite easy, if you have got it, to write a cheque for some cause you favour, but it is very much harder to give yourself and your time to that cause as well, and much more generous. And since we are not perfect like God is, we give what we can.

There is, for most adults, something very wearying about preparations for Christmas. For myself I dread all the Christmas cards I have to send out and anxiously tick off those I receive against those I have despatched, nervous that I may have lost somebody's esteem to whom I have forgotten to send a card this year. And then I think of what a racket the Christmas card business is and the further expense of tips and presents. In fact one can work oneself up into such a state of self-pity about Christmas that one could hate the whole thing. Or one could take the Pharisaical attitude of being shocked at the secular nature of most Christmas cards – a line I am disposed to take myself – but really the most secular card from a commercial firm or printed good wishes from a Moslem to a Dialectical Materialist has the nature of a sacrament. They are a giving and an unwitting commemoration of the anniversary of the greatest gift of all.

How could God be understood except in terms of what you touch and see? And if it were not for Christmas and God becoming man, we should not be able to receive the gift of Himself any morning of the week in the consecrated bread and wine of Holy Communion.

Copyright acknowledgements

The publisher and author acknowledge with thanks permission to reproduce extracts from the following.

Every effort has been made to seek permission to use copyright material reproduced in this book. The publisher apologizes for those cases where permission might not have been sought and, if notified, will formally seek permission at the earliest opportunity.

Permission has been sought from the Estate of Sir John Betjeman, care of Aitken Alexander Agency, for all the extracts reproduced in this book, except those detailed below. In addition, permission has been sought from and granted by the various copyright holders of the remaining pieces (as detailed below):

Extract from *Summoned by Bells* (John Murray, 1960): reproduced by permission of John Murray Publishers.

'The fabric of our faith', from *Punch* (23 December 1953): reproduced by permission of Punch Limited.

'The church Union as Defender of the Faith', from *Church Times* (27 June 1958): reproduced by permission of the *Church Times*.

'Gordon Square church', from *The University Church of Christ the King: A Brief History* (1964): reproduced by permission of the University of London Chaplaincy; permission also sought from the Estate of Sir John Betjeman.

'The Grosvenor Chapel', Introduction to *Godly Mayfair* , ed. Ann Callender (1980): reproduced by permission of Ann Callender.

'On marriage', from *Moral Problems: Questions on Christianity with Answers by Prominent Churchmen* (Mowbray, 1952): reproduced by kind permission of Continuum International Publishing Group.

'Christmas from St Martin's', from *St Martin's Christmas Matinée* (1960): reproduced by permission of the clergy of St Martin-in-the-Fields, London.

Index of churches

Index of names and subjects

190